# HOW TO ACE YOUR DEGREE

Inspired by Student Success Stories, We Tell You What Your Tutors Don't

A. RAJA

Published by Academic Underdogs Ltd



Printed in the United Kingdom

*Cover design by SJR*

First Printing, 2019

ISBN 978-0-9933488-3-9

How to ACE Your Degree
Roberts House, 2 Manor Rd, Ruislip, Middlesex HA4 7LB

www.AcademicUnderdogs.com

# Contents

## Execution – Efficient Learning



## Motivation – Getting to the Table and Staying There



## Looking Ahead

## Preface

"Why do you always look tired?"

The highest performing student in my year group, Danny, glared at me with a quizzical smile fixed on his face. I looked tired because I *was* tired. I look tired because I had just pulled my 8$^{th}$ 'all-nighter' in 6 weeks.

I was struggling to manage my time, to balance degree work with social commitments while warding off distractions. Danny, on the other hand, looked fresh as a daisy. He had completed his work a day before the deadline, just as he'd done all year. To celebrate, he was heading out to a society social he'd somehow managed to organise while simultaneously cruising to a deadline that had turned the rest of my group into extras from Dawn of the Dead. Everyone else was preparing to call it a night and crawl into whatever abyss they could find; Danny's day was just beginning.

Danny left with a broad smile on his face and an equally cheery girl on his arm. "Don't you just hate people like that?" one of my friends said when Danny departed. "They seem to have everything figured out. No stress, no worries; they're like robots."

It was then that something dawned on me: The gap between who I was and who I wanted to be had grown too large. I realised that I wasn't going to get through my degree and land a decent job unless I fixed this broken pattern. I needed to change, to escape the rut I was in. I needed to be more like Danny.

This realisation was all I needed to kick-start a series of improvements. I achieved a first-class honours degree, an award from the dean of students for having one of the highest degree scores in my year group, and multiple internship/job offers.

Every now and again, we all need perspective. A reminder of why we're doing what we're doing; a belief that we can get there and a strategy to get the job done. *How to ACE Your Degree* will provide you with all this and more.

# Chapter 1
# Who Am I?

You know those skinny Indian kids who look like they are too young to have a moustache? That was me in my teens. It's fair to say that I didn't sit highly on the social food chain. This would have been OK if I was a straight A student – I would have endured a few crappy years of high school before moving onto an awesome career and a future filled with money and women. Unfortunately, I wasn't academic either.

After leaving high school with mediocre GCSEs, I began my A-Levels with a new-found determination. I was committed to my work and my future – convinced I was doing enough to succeed. I worked my backside off, but when my results came in my hard work was rewarded with little more than Ds and Us.

I can laugh about it now, but those grades really hurt. I wanted nothing more than to get As & Bs and secure a place at a top university. This was the turning point for me. I was fed-up of failing and receiving sympathetic pats on the back. I realized that hard work and determination wasn't enough to get me through so, after speaking with a number of successful students, I created a strategy to improve my grades.

Goals and plans were nothing new to me. I'd made plenty of them before without acting on them, but this time it was different. My A-Level results left me with a chip on my shoulder that remained for the entire year. I wanted to prove everyone wrong, so I worked almost every day and executed my study strategy. This time, when results day rolled around, I was able to walk away with my head held high thanks to a succession of straight As and module marks above 90%. It was one of the biggest transformations my teachers had ever seen and it shocked my parents and friends.

**University**

With a packed Toyota, my parents dropped me at my halls in Kings Cross and the university experience began. I introduced myself to a few people in my building and we spent the morning knocking on every room to introduce ourselves, going from one door to the next and shaking hundreds of hands.

The first day set the tone for the entire year. My social media accounts exploded overnight and grew exponentially from there; I dated more girls than I had ever even spoken to in high school, and I became involved with a society.

Unfortunately, I was so preoccupied with having a good time and socialising, that I lost track with my coursework and tests. The good habits I had developed from my A-Levels faded away. Every evening that I returned from lectures I would laze around with friends, watching movies and procrastinating. I said 'yes' pretty much every time someone asked if I wanted to hang out.

Do you want to play football with the Maths and Econ guys? Yes.

Do you want to go to Vodka Revs on Monday night? Yes

Do you want to go down to do laundry? Yes.

I can't open this strawberry jam. Can you help? YES!

I got my head into gear 2-3 months before exams and pulled together a 2:1 with an overall mark of 65%. Luckily, as the year only counted towards 15% of my degree, this wasn't a complete disaster. However, I couldn't help but feel rather disappointed by the grade. You're probably picturing the 'world's smallest violin' playing me a sad song, but you have to understand that transforming my fortunes during A-Levels felt like coming back to win after being 6-0 down in the Champions League final.

After all that effort, I knew what the phrase 'hard work' meant and understood the level of self-discipline required to succeed. Why didn't I do something about my attitude? I couldn't let myself fall back into that hole again.

### The Summer that Changed my Life

During the summer of my first year, I met with my biological brother (long story) at a family wedding in Toronto. We shared a room together for 4 days and he gave me an insight into his life after university. After working for Shell, he started an import and export business and became a millionaire aged 23. The business eventually tanked and he lost 90% of his fortune. With the little money he had left, he founded a trading business that speculated on foreign currencies.

He used programming knowledge he had acquired at university to build algorithms which automatically bought and sold currency pairs. He showed me the algorithm in action, including how much money he was making each month and his track record over the past few years. He was clearly successful and after hooking up with the hottest girl at the wedding, I thought he was an absolute legend! His success showed me what was possible if I got my act together. More importantly, his influence gave me two important gifts: direction and inspiration. I finally knew what industry and type of job I wanted to pursue after university.

**Second and Final Year**

My final two years counted for 85% of my total grade, so the reality check from the previous year and the inspiration I received over the summer couldn't have come at a better time. I made a commitment to find good work experience at a top brand and do everything necessary to achieve an average of 75%.

After speaking to several successful students and alumni, I quickly realised where I was going wrong. I was treating my degree like my A-Levels, even though the system was very different. The rules of the game had changed. Exam boards no longer defined the syllabus and determined our marks, my lecturers did. You can't coast through university and then bury your head in a textbook during exams. Also, I failed to collaborate with or learn from anyone else. Top students know that their peers and lecturers were their greatest assets. I realised that having a network of 'specialists' helped me find relevant information and learn faster; leaving me with more time to socialise with friends and look for jobs.

These revelations not only improved my grades, but also the efficiency in which I obtained them. Not a single person in my year group was able to secure a good job/internship and achieve a first at the same time. Most were forced to enrol on a Masters course out of necessity rather than choice because they spent too much time working and failed to invest any time into job hunting. This might sound a little arrogant, but my approach got me everything I wanted and it's the reason I feel qualified to write this book.

# Chapter 2
# Who I Think you Are

So, that's me. Now, who are you?

Vegan, CrossFit enthusiast, indifferent about Brexit, Donald Trump fan? Don't worry, I'm not going to read you your Horoscope. Instead, I'm going to tell you who I think you *might* be and who I think you *should* be, assuming you want to leave university with your head held high, that is. That's what this book is really about: Becoming a well-rounded person who is confident in their own ability and has the grades/accolades to prove it.

Right now, I'd guess you are currently a $6^{th}$ form student or recently liberated A-level/BTEC/IB student who has just finished their exams and wants to know how to make the most out of university. You could also be a university student who doesn't want thousands of pounds worth of tuition fees to go to waste.

Regardless of your age or level of education, you are someone who sees the value in having a solid game plan, strategy or direction. Seeing the bigger picture is important to you and that's what I aim to provide with the *Level Up Series* and this book in particular.

# Chapter 3
# Who this Book Definitely is For

While I believe that most university students will benefit from my advice, the core audience for this book are those who are ambitious but struggle to avoid distractions and focus on important tasks. Usually, these individuals didn't perform as well as they hoped to in 6th form or college. As a rule of thumb, if you achieved anything less than 120 UCAS points, this book will probably add a lot of value to your life.

Nevertheless, there are plenty of students who smash college and fall flat on their face at university because they find it difficult to adjust. If you're in this boat and feel that you might tumble over the edge, I can help. Every year I'm contacted by straight A/A* students who want to check or refine their approach.

### Will this Book Apply to the Subject I'm Taking?

As someone who has always been interested in education, whenever I meet someone new, I naturally annoy them with questions like, 'How did you achieve a first? What did you do differently from everyone else? Did you change your study strategy from college? How did you decide what to do after university? How can I get a job like yours?

## Who this book definitely is for

It's not the ideal topic of conversation for the smoking section of a night club, but I can't help myself! All these conversations, combined with research/polling I've conducted, have uncovered five important facts.

1. **As you move through the educational food chain, from primary to secondary to university, your strategy should change.**

This may seem obvious, but you'll be surprised at how many students smash their GCSEs/A-Levels/BTEC/IB and then fail at university. As your educational environment changes, so should your strategy.

2. **All educational institutions are made of the same stuff.**

Even though most universities and subjects have different eco-systems, every educational institution is pretty much run in the same way. You have lectures, lecturers, tutors, alumni, co-students, exams, past exam papers, coursework, syllabuses, textbooks, hand-outs, etc. Succeeding in an educational institution, or any institution for that matter, comes down to using the resources around you to learn quickly and outperform your peers. There are hacks everywhere. I'll show you mine and teach you how to find your own. You can carry these techniques into any post-graduate course and even into the workplace.

3. **When you enter an educational institution with the aim to get something out of it, like a degree, there is always an efficient way of getting the job done.**

Students who don't succeed tend to put a lot of time and energy into activities which don't help them achieve their end goal. You are there to do a job and complete a goal, and every minute you spend focusing on something other than this job will take you further away from completing that goal.

4. **Students who find the most 'efficient path' tend to do well in university and life.**

It's always good to ask yourself, 'Am I on the right track?' Asking yourself this question and searching for the answer is a good habit to have and will give you an edge for the rest of your life.

5. **The 'efficient way' is the same for every course and every institution.**

To ensure I've covered all angles, I have enlisted the help of current and ex-students who have studied a variation of subjects, including Maths, Economics, Business Management, Medicine, Dentistry, Political Sciences and English, as well as most engineering disciplines and most sciences. These students have gone to universities across the country.

# Chapter 4
# **Who This Book Isn't For**

If you are not hungry to succeed, to improve your life and to be a better version of yourself, then this book probably isn't for you. As the saying goes, 'You can't help people who don't want to be helped.' You need to have a drive to succeed and do better. Over the years, I've helped many different students with different personalities. If they were anxious and nervous, I helped them manage their emotions better; if they were continuously second-guessing themselves and confused about how they should revise, I gave them direction; if they were stuck in a rut and always procrastinating, I broke them out of their cycle.

However, if they had no hunger then I struggled to make an impact. No matter how much I tried to convince them that they were in control of their future, it just didn't work. Luckily, these are the minority and most e-mails that land in my inbox are from people who want to improve. The fact that you have clicked on the preview screen on Amazon or bought this book already tells me you're not one of these people.

Even if you have the smallest flame in your belly, I can grow it and get you to believe in yourself. I can give you a game plan to achieve the highest grades possible without sacrificing all the other important experiences of university.

# Chapter 5
# Is a Degree Really That Important?

Higher education is overrated. The marginal benefit of education decreases as the level of education increases. If a kid quits school aged 7 they're going to be at a big disadvantage compared to a kid that quits at 10. However, the difference between a 17 and a 21-year-old giving up education isn't nearly as significant.

Unless you are doing Medicine or other specialist subjects, by the time you reach 18, you've pretty much learned all you need to know. Anything you learn beyond that age is generally useless and will be forgotten after graduating. Degree coursework isn't harder than A-level material, it just goes into more detail and you won't need most of those details.

At this age you are educated enough to think critically and solve problems and you have the basic skills to qualify for most graduate jobs. Unfortunately, most employers don't realise this or have no other way to separate weak and strong candidates. It is for this and other historical reasons that society has decided you need a degree to qualify for a job. Even though the information you learn doesn't matter, your grades still do.

## Is a Degree Really That Important?

Whether you want to study for a Masters or join a company, you will need a minimum grade, usually a 2:1, so don't use my previous remarks as an excuse to take your foot off the gas. There is work to be done.

Without exam boards, a syllabus and the structure that school provides, many find achieving good grades challenging. But it's not very difficult if you know what you're doing and there is always an efficient way of getting the marks you need. I have several techniques and an effective strategy that will help you ACE any degree you are studying.

# Chapter 6

# Plans After University & Why They Matter

UK employers care about the quality and ranking of your university but not about the course you study. In other countries, such as the US, if you study Chemistry you're expected to become a chemist. If you don't want to be a chemist and would rather be a lawyer, you have to study law for a few years before applying to a law firm.

Luckily, here in the UK, we can change our minds! Even if you're studying a specialist subject like Medicine, you can still apply for and land a graduate position at an investment bank. You have more choices than you probably realise. There are plenty of postgraduate courses available too, and many people 'upgrade' to a better university to boost their CV.

With all these choices, indecision can creep in. This is normal but as I'll explain below, you can't stay in this state for too long. Let's look at a few scenarios:

**Scenario 1: Do you want to do a postgraduate course? Are you doing a specialist degree and know that you will be entering the same industry as your degree?**

For example, if you're studying medicine, are you set on becoming a doctor/surgeon/GP or any other profession in medicine? If so, passing your degree would take priority over anything else and you can start job hunting towards the end of your course. The same applies if you want to enrol on a postgraduate course in any field of study.

**Scenario 2: What if you know what you want to do after university and are doing a degree unrelated to that industry?**

For example, you want to work in a tech start-up and are studying theology. Under this scenario, you will need to start career hunting from your first year and invest significantly more time into it than someone who wants to be a theology professor. Without a doubt, there will be times where you need to prioritise job hunting over your degree work.

**Scenario 3: What if you don't have a clue what to do after university?**

If you don't know what you want to do by the end of first year university, it's worth investing some time into solving this. You will graduate before you know it (scary, I know) and the earlier you figure this out, the more time you have to see what works and to change your mind. This is discussed in more detail in *How to Land Your Dream Graduate Job* but deciding what you want to do is an iterative and time-intensive process. Therefore, you can't start career hunting in your third year of university and this means your schedule will be different from most people in your course.

Let's say you're doing Mechanical Engineering but aren't sure if you want to be a Mechanical Engineer. Your 4 best friends in your course are pretty sure they want to get a job in engineering but they aren't focused on graduate jobs now and are spending most of their time doing coursework. You can't follow their schedule! Those who have chosen their career can get away with spending 60% of their overall time on degree work, 20% career hunting and 20% on social. If you haven't decided, then your schedule will be closer to 50%-35%-15%.

If you are in group 2 or 3, your schedule must be different to everyone else's. That's why you can't copy your peers or 'go with the herd' as you might have done at college. You also can't measure your productivity against anyone else's.

Have you ever asked someone how far they've gotten with a piece of work only to find out that they are nearly finished, while you haven't even started? You feel the pressure and do your best to catch up. That reactive approach can't exist at university, especially if you need more time career searching.

This can be tough to manage and a little lonely at times. For example, when your 4 best friends are taking their time on coursework having completed 50% of the work in 2 weeks, you will need to have done 60-70% of it. When they are planning to go out on a bender after the deadline, but you have an internship interview lined up the next day, you may need to pass. These small sacrifices are difficult but necessary.

In all scenarios, it's advisable to get some part-time experience – check out *How to Land Your Dream Graduate Job*.

# Chapter 7
# What's to Come

Over the next few chapters, we are going to dive into 'The Ultimate University Game Plan'. This is the formula I used to achieve one of the highest degree scores in my faculty. It has been utilised by thousands of undergraduates that I've mentored over the past few years and has proven successful time and time again.

This game plan is split into two parts: Strategy and Execution. In the first part, I'll show you when and what to revise; in the second I'll show you how to revise. By the end of these two sections, you will have a step-by-step plan on how to achieve top grades.

Towards the end of this book, in the 'Motivation' section, I'll describe how you can stay productive throughout the year and keep distractions at bay.

# The Ultimate University Game Plan

# Chapter 8
# Hold your Own Intervention

"Where is the next lecture?"

I received this text from Ed, one of my friends at UCL, while at university. It's a harmless question that every student has asked at some point, but this wasn't the first time that Ed had asked me it.

Ed had a problem; he was reactive. This reactive nature impacted every facet of his life, from his social life to his studies. He was disorganised, constantly playing catch-up and never quite operating on the same playing field as everyone else. Unfortunately, but not unexpectedly, Ed didn't get the grades he wanted and had to drop out early.

I never judged Ed because I had been in his shoes during first year and multiple times prior to that. During my first year at university, I became more reactive than I wanted to be and was sick and tired of leaving my coursework to the last minute. To break myself out of it, I tried something different.

It was Saturday morning and I had until Monday morning to deliver a project that I had barely begun. Usually, I would have forced myself to pull an all-nighter on Sunday to get the work done. But I was so angry at myself for the attitude I had developed that I forced myself to do the all-nighter on Saturday night instead. I ended up pulling 2 all-nighters in a row, going 48 hours without a wink of sleep.

After I handed the project in, one of my friends caught me having a mental breakdown in the toilet and I was forced to face the reality that my sloppy, reactive nature had caused. It was an emotionally draining and traumatising experience.

My double all-nighter acted as an intervention and is exactly what I needed. I realised that without any pressure and the fear of failing if I missed the deadline, I would never get anything done! It helped me snap out of this reactive habit and I became very organised and proactive over the weeks that followed.

**Are you a Proactive Person?**

Do you need external pressure to complete tasks on time or can you finish with time left to check your work? Do you find yourself asking others for help a lot? Are you organised with your time or do you forget important dates quite easily? Do you like to plan ahead or go with the flow? Take a moment to answer these questions, grab a pencil and draw a mark on the scale below to show where you think are.

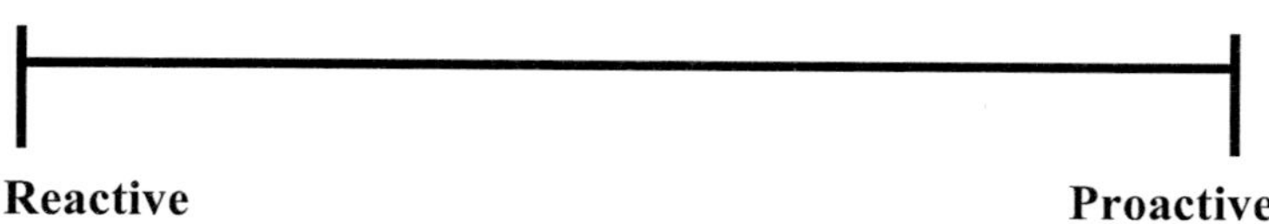

**Reactive** **Proactive**

This isn't the most detailed way of determining how reactive and proactive you are. I'm sure there are plenty of psychometric tests that can assess this, but I don't feel they are needed. From mentoring thousands of students, I've found that everyone knows where they sit on this scale.

If you're being honest and your mark was on the right of the scale, congratulations! Keep up the attitude and follow my guidance closely. If your mark is on the left, your work ethic is broken and you need to fix this otherwise no amount of guidance will help.

I wish I could sit here and give you some techniques to help you become more proactive but there are none. This quality comes from sustained changes you make in your day-to-day habits. Being proactive in one area of your life can have an effect on others. For example, if Ed simply got to grips with his schedule and knew where and when his lectures were, this would have a positive effect and make him less reactive in other areas like completing coursework on time. In addition to small sustained changes you can also create occasional large changes, not unlike my double-all-nighter.

### How to Hold your Own Solo-Intervention

When you're dating someone who keeps hurting your feelings and betraying your trust, your friends hold an intervention. At school, if your grades are dropping and not improving, your parents and teachers bring you in and tell you to fix up. At university, there might be a tutor around to give you a nudge, but there is no one there to grab you by the scruff of the neck and tell you to sort your life out. Your mistakes and your flaws are your problem and you need to hold a solo-intervention to fix them.

A solo-intervention can take many forms. One of my mentees handed his phone to a friend for a week, stocked up his fridge with food and sat at his desk until he finished his project. Another friend of mine left the country without notice and cocooned herself somewhere for several days to kickstart her revision. One of my mentees was spending too much time on social media. I asked her to be honest with herself and download an app to track her results and this made her realise just how much time she was wasting on Instagram and Snapchat. Whatever you decide to do, it has to involve stepping outside your comfort zone and breaking the pattern of your daily life.

# Chapter 9
# 90-10 Rule

The difference between proactive and inactive people is that the former always likes to know they are moving in the right direction while the latter just idly meanders on whatever course they can find. A proactive person will stop and check every now and then to make sure they are on course, but they won't waste time second guessing themselves. 90% of the time, they have their head down and are executing their plan. 10% of the time, they lift their head to look where they're going. Remind yourself of this ratio if you start chopping and changing your plan too much. Hopefully, after reading The Ultimate University Game Plan you will have a *strategy* you believe in and the tools you need to *execute* this strategy.

**Strategy – 10%**

With my previous books, many students improved their grades by following my strategy closely. However, at undergraduate level, you may need to use this as a guide rather than a biblical game plan.

In a nutshell, my strategy involves:

1) Building a network of specialists from your year group that you can call upon for help or trade information with. It may sounds a little 'MI5', but I assure you this can be the most effective way to secure top exam and coursework scores without spending hours doing research.

2) Using your network and research to determine your learning materials before anyone else.

3) Creating a learning timetable to ensure you absorb and retain all the material before your exams.

4) Putting the strategy into place.

**Execution – 90%**

Once you have a strategy in place, you need to execute it. Of course, taking action and maintaining it is the hard part. I can't count how many times I've made plans, strategies, set goals and forgotten about them a few days later. The key is to keep trying until you get into a rhythm. Then, use every trick in the book to ensure you stay in that rhythm for as long as possible. In the execution section, I'll show you a special approach to preparing for your exams that I have perfected and trialled on hundreds of students who have subsequently succeeded.

**90-10 Rule**

I can't help but reiterate that this will work, and perseverance is key. All the guidance I provide to you helped me achieve one of the highest scores in my year group and helped countless others achieve similar results. My 3-step approach will work in the majority of cases but you may need to adapt it depending on the requirements of your course.

# Strategy – What Top Performers Don’t Tell you

# Chapter 10
# Building your Network of Specialists

In 2008 Facebook's CTO, Adam D'Angelo, quit his job and whipped-up a media storm in the process. Although it wasn't public knowledge at the time, his departure had a purpose. He wanted to start working on a 'question and answer' website called Quora. Two years after being released to the public, his new project was generating 1.5 million unique views per month. As of today, Quora is receiving 200 million monthly unique visitors and is worth over $1.8 billion.

When asked why he created Quora, Adam said:

*"The knowledge available by talking to people in any given field vastly exceeds the knowledge available on the internet."*

In other words, Google can't answer all your questions! On D'Angelo's platform, those who wanted information would ask questions like, 'How do I tell my boyfriend that I don't love him anymore?' or 'How do I split shares with my business partners?'

Many people from different backgrounds would then post answers to these questions, from a relationship councillor with

20 years of experience to a successful multi-millionaire or corporate lawyer. People get a chance to up-vote the answers they feel are the best or most useful. Quite often, the best and most truthful answers make it to the top of the page. This shows that people can instinctively tell when someone knows what they are talking about. Quora would not be a multi-billion-pound company if this assumption wasn't true.

To succeed at university and beyond, you need to become a walking-talking Quora. By asking the right questions to the right people, you will instinctively 'up-vote' the answers that are true and find information faster. This is a very different approach to what you are probably used to.

Finding information is easy at college. Everything you needed was probably in a textbook and if it wasn't, it was just a YouTube video or Google search away. University work isn't more complicated than college, it's just more detailed and specialised. The more specialised a subject is, the less information there is out there to help you understand it and the harder it is to find that information.

One of my mentees, Melissa, learned this the hard way.

**Meet Melissa**

Melissa was a first-year physics student at a London university. She was a few months into her course and struggling when she came to me for help.

**Me:** *"How's it going so far?"*

**Melissa**: *"Not been easy to be honest. We've already had a few important coursework submissions and graded tests. I'm finding it so much harder than college."*

**Me:** *"Why?"*

**Melissa**: *"Every time a piece of work is set, I'm just left stumped. The lecture notes and recommended reading aren't extensive enough for me to even attempt the work. There's just so much analysis and reading in-between the lines needed. I can't find the information online either."*

**Me:** *"Now that you're studying something specialised, the internet will only get you so far. Let's say you're attempting a coursework question and search for the topic on Google. Google's algorithms will probably point you to a page that gives you a broad explanation of the topic. This is because most people don't need the level of detail that you need, and Google is designed to provide search results useful to most people.*

*Search engines do a great job of getting you 90% of the way there but sometimes that critical 10% you need to answer a coursework question remains hidden deep on the 22nd page of a Google search result or in the corner of a textbook bought on Amazon."*

**Melissa**: *"So what do you suggest I do?"*

**Me**: *"Your chances of success and efficiency improve if you can find people who can point you in the right direction. You need to build a network of specialists."*

**Who are your Specialists?**

"Did you use this textbook for that piece of coursework?"

"How do I get this professor to give me their time?"

"Are these projects taking me too long to complete?"

"What type of questions does this lecturer set in exams?"

Specialists are people who can provide good answers to these and the thousands of other questions you will have during university. In order of importance, your specialists at university should be:

1. Students from the years above.
2. Ambitious people in your year.
3. Lecturers, Tutors and Professors.

**Students From the Year Above**

"How do you know all these people?"

Remember my friend Danny, who achieved the highest mark in the year? I asked him the above question a few months into first year after I saw him having a laugh with a few people from the year above. He initially shrugged his shoulders but as our friendship grew, he described that he had strategically formed these relationships.

Students from the year above have the obvious advantage of having completed the work you are currently doing. All it takes is a point in the right direction or a quick tip from a conversation in the lift to save you hours of time and boost your grades. If you play your cards right, some of them may even sacrifice their time to explain difficult concepts or help you navigate arduous areas of your subject.

Not all of them will be friendly and willing to help, but some of them will be and it's your job to find them. When you do, use everything you learnt from *How to be Admired and Respected* to build rapport with them. Build the relationships to a level where they stop you in the corridor to have a quick chat or where you can pick up the phone and call them. Be respectful of their time, always show appreciation and reciprocate favours. This will be a skill you take forward with you throughout your life, with friends, family and especially in your career.

**Melissa:** *"Why would anyone bother to help me?"*

**Me:** *"You'll be surprised how helpful others are if you can simply summon up the courage to ask. Those social barriers between year groups in school and college don't really exist at* *university. Don't be afraid to show your ambition, talk to everyone and smile. People will help you!"*

**How do I Get in Touch with the Year Above?**

An introduction through someone you already know is the most effective way to start a relationship. However, if that's not possible, hang around in the common areas of your department. This was my personal favourite way of meeting people from the year above. Most of the time, I'd look over my shoulder at people sitting behind me and start a conversation. On one occasion, I kept my work on the desk and the person next to me recognised it and said, 'I remember doing that'. We then struck up a conversation, he answered some important questions and we ended up speaking quite regularly.

Many people in the year above will list their textbooks for sale – purchase them and use the opportunity to strike up a conversation. Ask if you can have their old notes. If you don't ask, you don't get. There may even be some hand-scribbled notes or guidance in there.

Course societies and meetups are also great ways to network. By having a position of responsibility in the society as a treasurer or president, you will have a lot of close interactions with the year above.

Regardless of how you choose to network with other year groups, eliminate any shyness and be proactive about building these relationships over time. Like a picture or click 'follow' on social media; smile while passing in the corridor; say 'hello' on the bus.

**Ambitious People in your Year Group**

Over time, a hierarchy will form in your year group and cliques will be established. This is a huge generalisation, but everyone in your year will typically fall into one of 4 categories:

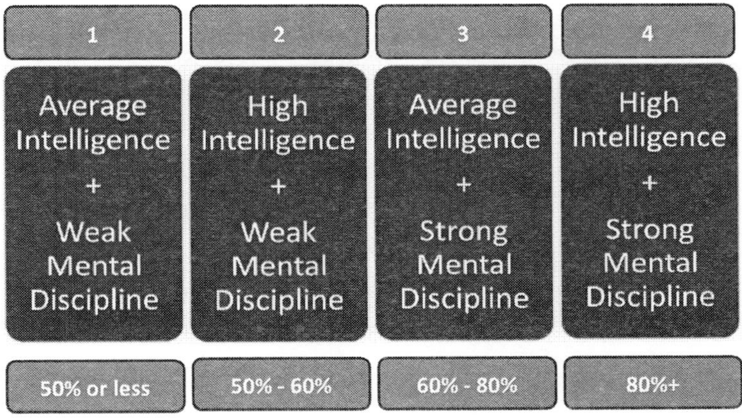


If you truly want to succeed and achieve the highest grades possible, you not only need to be in circles 3 and 4; you also need to know others in those circles. Trust me – it will make your life a lot easier.

Within those circles, there will be the ultra-intelligent individuals who learn quickly and those who seem to have a knack or specialism for particular subjects. It will be very easy to spot the former group of individuals, and if you're already at university you will probably know who they are. Keep them close! The latter group of people are harder to identify and you will need to keep an eye out for them. In my course, there was a subject called 'Fluid Dynamics'. One of the quietest girls in my year group, who barely spoke to anyone and never raised her hand in lectures, had already studied this subject back home in China. She was very good and became my specialist in that subject. Without making the effort to speak to her, I would have never known!

**Lecturers, Tutors and Professors**

Your course staff are the last group of specialists you need to build relationships with but they are surprisingly the least helpful. This is partly because they are juggling both their teaching obligations and their academic research. Some professors can be teaching hundreds of undergrads, so the teacher-student ratio isn't as good as it was at school or college. In addition to this, professors can have a few research students and PHDs under their wing so undergrads can seem like annoying toddlers continuously tugging on their leg.

Regardless of how busy, unhelpful or standoffish your professors may seem; **you need to speak to them**. You'd be surprised how many undergrads go an entire year, sometimes the entire length of their course, never speaking one-on-one with their lecturers. These people not only teach but create your syllabus and exam papers! It may be today, tomorrow, next month or next year but they will eventually drop hints about your final exam. You need to be around to catch them.

Learn their schedules, busy periods and whether they are morning or evening people. Again, use everything you learnt in *How to be Admired and Respected* to build rapport with course staff. They will never admit it, but they are human and have their favourite students. Make sure you are one of them!

**Trading Information**

At university, information is a valuable commodity. Your specialists are your suppliers of this commodity, and just like a marketplace, you can trade information with others. Danny was a master at this.

Danny would always take a crack at coursework or revision questions himself and get an idea of what information he needed. He would then identify the gaps in his knowledge and use textbooks or lecture hand-outs to help him understand. He wouldn't always understand everything on his own, but when he failed to grasp something he would just pick up a phone and tap into his trade information. He would call his specialists in the subject and trade information and solutions. Often, he would take information obtained from specialists and trade that with other specialists in other subjects. Danny essentially became an information hustler.

This enabled him to consistently achieve top marks in his coursework and exams. He was always first to find the information and therefore first to complete the work. This gave him time to check and refine it. While most were rushing to complete work on the morning of the deadline, Danny would be adding small icons, infographics and various type fonts to make his work stand out. This was his trademark and the lecturers loved it.

Danny was not the most intelligent person in our year group and he was honest about that. His edge was in building relationships and being resourceful. He cleverly built a network of 'specialists', lecturers and older students and then leveraged this network to produce the highest standard of work.

I eventually understood what Danny was doing and came to some major conclusions. I knew I couldn't treat university like it was 6th form and accepted that this was a completely different playing field. During second year, I built my own network of specialists, including Danny. I soon realised that although people are willing to help you, it's important to have something tangible to offer them in return.

## Be a Specialist to Others

As you settle into university, there will be one or more subjects that you intrinsically enjoy and have a knack for. Double-down on those subjects and become a specialist in them. This will give you something to offer others. My specialist subject was 'Transport Processes'. I prioritised this subject and was always first to finish coursework or test preparation for it. Then I helped others if they were struggling.

Later, I became an expert in everything related to graduate job applications, which of course is completely unrelated to

Chemical Engineering. Towards the tail end of the course, my whole year group became focused on finding internships and jobs. I had started this process very early and had some good experience already. People came to me for help with their applications, CVs and psychometric tests. If you asked my friends what I was good at, they would have said, graduate applications and Transport Processes. Being a specialist gave me something to offer others and, in turn, they never hesitated to help me when I asked. Trading help and information in this way enabled me to complete work efficiently.

The way I've described all this implies that I'm going up to people saying:

*'If I give you the answers to my interview questions at JP Morgan, will you help me with my design project?'*

That's not how it goes. Initially, I helped people without expectation but with a 'mutual agreement' that they'd help me in the future. However, it wasn't long before some of these, 'I scratch your back and you scratch mine' acquaintances turned into genuine friends. When the trust was established, we stopped keeping an internal balance of favours and helped each other out because we were mates.

A year and a half into university, my handful of close friends were the most ambitious people in our year group. Our final grades were a country mile from everyone else's, and we all carried this work ethic into postgrad. Three of my friends went to Oxford and Imperial to do Masters. We all landed good graduate jobs and internships at top companies. Two of us started our own businesses and no longer need to work for anyone else. Because of our shared ambition and selfless friendship, these people are still some of my closest friends.

Would I have achieved a first if I didn't have this support network? This sounds a little arrogant, but yes, I believe so. However, it would have taken a hell of a lot more work and, most importantly, time. Time I'd much rather spend finding a job or going out and enjoying university life!

**Melissa:** *"Isn't this cheating?"*

There is a fine line between 'learning from each other' and plagiarism. You should never blindly copy someone else's work as you will only be cheating yourself. Top performers learn from others but don't plagiarise. You're going to need to understand the information for your exams anyway. Also, gathering information and understanding concepts quickly is an important life skill. Those who take matters into their own hands tend to be more original and proactive. You can't get ahead in life by copying everyone all the time.

## Building your Network of Specialists

After university, there will be no textbook for life, and you will need to become efficient at finding information for tasks, such as deciding which house to buy or asking your new employer for a pay rise. You need to piece together information from various sources to make the best choice. Unless artificial intelligence improves, **a specialist in any given area will help you find and learn the relevant information much faster than any other resource.**

# Chapter 11
# What to Study?

Humans are resourceful creatures capable of learning great things with a little time and will. If I dropped you on a deserted island with nothing but a few textbooks and some marked papers, there's a good chance you would be an A* student in that particular subject within a few months. People don't always agree with me when I tell them this and teachers absolutely hate me for saying it, but it's true.

I am living breathing proof that for most courses, you don't need a teacher to succeed. In my second year of college I had to complete two years' worth of work in just one year, so I didn't have time to go to lectures. I had to move faster than my teachers because of the number of retakes I had. Otherwise I wouldn't have been able to complete my revision on time. I created my own learning schedule using only textbooks, hand-outs and past papers. Many of my final marks were in the high 90s and I beat many peers who had attended every lesson.

Therefore, I can confidently say that for most modules, I achieved my final scores because of resources outside the classroom, mainly textbooks and past papers. My story isn't unique, and ever since I wrote my first two books, I've been contacted by others who have achieved top grades without attending a single lesson. This all changes at university.

At university, you might be lucky enough to find one or two resources that cover everything you need for your final exam. I call these 'verified textbooks or learning materials'. These are materials that, when read front-to-back, can help you achieve 80% or more in an exam.

**Verified Textbooks or Learning Materials**

It's rare to have a resource like this at University. To put things into perspective, out of thirty modules I studied at university, only one had a verified textbook because it was written by my lecturer. I did better in this subject compared with others because I didn't need to look elsewhere.

**How to Verify your Textbook**

**Step One:** Find out who wrote the textbook

a. Did your lecturer or anyone associated with your lecturer write or co-write the textbook?

**Step Two:** Check the textbook itself:

a. Check the publishing date of your textbook (usually on the first 2-3 pages). Was it published less than 5 years ago?

**Step Three:** If you've been given a course structure or learning specification from your lecturer or tutor, compare it with your textbook:

a. Do the key learning outcomes in the specification match up with the heading and subheadings in the textbook?

If the answers to step two and three are yes, you probably have a core textbook. Things are looking good! However, you still need to double check with your lecturer.

**Step Four:** Ask your lecturer the following questions:

a. Does this textbook cover the entire learning specification?
b. If I learn this textbook front to back will I know enough to achieve 80% in the exam?

If the answers in step two to four are yes, then it's time for a fist pump! This means your textbook is indeed a 'verified textbook' and is the only resource (along with past papers) you need to achieve a first.

This should be your bible right up until exams and providing you use my study techniques, you'll have a great chance of achieving a top grade. However, if steps one to four indicate that your textbook is out of date or not designed for your course, then a little more detective work is needed before you can prepare for any exams.

## What if There is no Verified Textbook?

Chances are, you won't have a verified textbook and will need to piece all the information together from various sources. This is annoying because it will drain more time and make your life harder. However, it is a blessing in disguise because there aren't going to be any verified textbooks after you leave university. There will be no definitive guide to help you choose which property you should purchase, how to negotiate your salary or who you should marry. When you start working, you need to develop quick ways to find the information you need and have processes to learn 'on the job'. University has a lot of pointless aspects to it; however, it does provide a good stepping-stone to the working world.

**Melissa:** *"I followed your procedure and checked with my professors. There are no verified textbooks, but there are recommended books – should I just use these?"*

**Me:** *"If there is no verified textbook, you will need to piece together all your learning resources to create a revision or learning pack."*

## Putting Together your Revision Pack

This is where your network of specialists, particularly friends from the year above, come in handy. They can show you what learning resources are most relevant. Ask the same questions to different people and compare the answers. Focus on questions like:

1. How did you prepare for this exam?

2. Did you use a textbook – if so, which one?
3. Were the handouts useful?
4. If you were to go back in time what would you do differently?

Sometimes getting information out of people is like getting blood from a stone. You have to detect when people are being vague and then push to find details without being annoying. Quite often, you simply need to ask broad questions and then let them speak. It's amazing how many golden nuggets you can uncover by asking that one extra question. After trying to get some information out of my friend from the year above, at the end of the conversation he said:

*"Oh, by the way, I just remembered that there is a great resource on this topic offered by an American University. I'll send you the link."*

This American course covered *everything* I needed and the questions helped me prepare for two graded tests. Had I not pushed a little, it would never have jogged his memory and I would never have found this golden nugget.

**Melissa:** *"If no one is willing to point me in the right direction, what should I do?"*

**Me:** *"If you're not getting much help from anyone, you should start with your past papers and work backwards."*

Most people go looking for exam papers a few weeks before exams. They don't feel they are needed until they start revising or departments don't distribute them early enough.

If you are in the latter situation, it's important that you find your past papers through other means. For example, asking specialists from the year above or approaching the university library. I once contacted several alumni over social media to get hold of a past papers. You can then use these past papers and your course structure as a road map for the whole year.

For example, let's say you are studying Chemistry and notice that a particular topic appears in every past paper since 2015. When that topic comes up in a lecture, you know to pay close attention and ask your lecturer questions like:

*"I want to understand this a little better – are there any other published papers or other resources where I can learn more and practice questions?"*

If you're lucky, they may point you to a resource they use to create their exam questions – it happens! Using your past papers in this way can help you piece together your learning resources. Your goal should be to assemble a pack of learning material that is ready for you to use several months before exams.

**Melissa:** *"How should I organise all these learning resources?"*

**Me:** *"You should have one core learning resource and additional resources that branch off from it."*

Think of your revision pack as a tree. Your core learning resource is the trunk because it contains the most amount of relevant information for your exams. This could be a recommended textbook but is most likely to be printed hand-outs or slides created by your department. Your core learning resource should contain 50% or more of the information you need for the exam. i.e. if you learnt it front to back, you could get at least 50% in the exam.

**Melissa:** *"How can I tell what percentage of the course my core learning resource covers?"*

**Me:** *"You can verify it in the same way you tried to verify your textbooks. I personally went to my lecturer, looked them in the eye and asked:*

*If I learn this front-to-back, what mark would I get in the exam?*

*I didn't leave until I got an answer then I asked the same question to friends/specialists from the year above."*

You will then need to supplement your core learning resource with additional relevant information. These are the branches of the tree. Use the internet, academic papers and other published material to fill the gaps in your knowledge.

**Melissa:** *"How should I organise all these learning resources?"*

**Me:** *"Instead of writing notes on separate paper, annotate your handouts with:*

1. *Additional information you pick up in lectures.*
2. *References to 'non-core' learning resources."*

**Me:** *"If you need to write additional notes on a separate piece of paper, staple it to your core learning resources so that you don't lose it."*

During lectures, you should aim to take the least number of notes possible. There are so many occasions where I've looked around me in a lecture and everyone is copying information from PowerPoint slides when all the information will be available later. Usually, this is because no one realises that the slides will be available later and no one can be bothered to ask. Quite often, people only take notes because everyone else is or because they are bored. Even if you can listen and write at the same time, it doesn't matter how good of a multi-tasker you are, truly absorbing and learning any information requires undivided attention. You are way better off listening and asking questions than copying slides.

Subsequently, use post-it notes to reference important parts of your textbooks. Some of my textbooks were 700 pages long and a fraction of the content was actually relevant to my course. Instead of learning everything, as I would have done at college, I would go on a fact-finding mission with a few friends with the help of our lecturer. Our mission was to discover which parts of the textbook were relevant. The reason we did it together, was because if I walked into a lecturer's office and asked them to spend an hour going through the textbook with me, they would have told me to 'do one' (which they did many times). Instead, each of us paid our lecturer a visit about five times over a month and took with us:

1. Course specification or structure.

2. Pad of post-it notes.
3. Pencil (obvs).
4. Recommended textbook(s).

We then asked them to highlight important parts we should learn and then reported back to each other.

I'm sure by now you might feel a few of my experiences and suggestions are a little over the top and downright strange. However, this is what it takes to succeed.

**Melissa:** *"Should I go to lectures?"*

**Me:** *"Only to those which are informative. If there is a lecturer who isn't engaging to the point that every ounce of will power can't get you to concentrate, there is no point sitting there and listening for 2 hours."*

**What to study?**

1. Ask your network (continuously).
2. Start with your past papers and learning specification and then work backwords.
3. Piece together your learning resources throughout the year.
4. Meticulously organise your various learning resources by choosing one core resource which points to several peripheral resources.
5. Make annotations rather than notes.

Second-guessing whether your learning materials are relevant will make you anxious and you'll end up cherry-picking information based on how you feel at that time. By putting together your learning packs in the way I described, you should be able to hold them and confidently say:

*"If I learn everything in my hands, I will achieve close to 90% in my exams."*

Then all you need to worry about is how and **when** you should learn it.

# Chapter 12
# **When to Study?**

*'What's the point of revising now if I'll forget everything before the exam anyway?'*

This was always my excuse for not revising at school and I still hear this from university students. Unless you're in the top percentile of intelligence, this is by far the most damaging assumption you can make.

It's hard to not believe any different, because information is so easy to forget. If in one month's time, I asked you to write down everything you remember from this book, you'd struggle to regurgitate even just 10%. This is why intense cramming before the exam seems like a logical approach.

The problem is, not everyone can get away with cramming. Very often, exams are bunched-up together either on the same day or on consecutive days. For a person who doesn't have a photographic memory, a few days is not enough to effectively retain all the information you need. You have to **learn in layers** and start earlier!

**Memory – The Virtual Filing Cabinet**

Our memories are like virtual filing cabinets. When you learn something for the first time, a fraction of that information is filed into place. Over time, the information in the filing cabinet shuffles around and becomes disorganised. However, when you re-learn the same set of information you add more to the file and reorganise it at the same time. After each repetition or layer, the more information you add and the longer it stays organised for. The graph below is an example of how applying 4 layers of learning over 40 days can help you retain close to 80% of what's required:

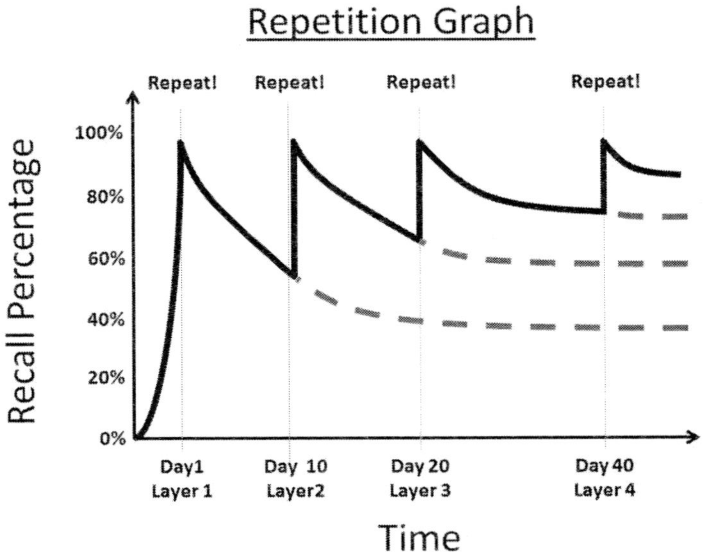

**Melissa:** *"I have a learning pack ready for one of my subjects. If I learn all of it, would that be my first layer completed?"*

**Me:** *"Yes. If you learn it using my study techniques (which I'll show you later) front-to-back, that's your first layer done for that particular subject."*

**Melissa:** *"Then, if I then go over the same learning pack using your study techniques a second time, that would be my second layer done?"*

**Me:** *"Yes."*

**Melissa:** *"Seems pretty straightforward. I need to put together a learning pack for each subject then revise everything in that pack a few times over before exams."*

**Me:** *"Exactly."*

**Melissa:** *"How many layers should I do for each subject?"*

**Me:** *"It depends on what you want to do after university. As a rule of thumb, you should complete at least one layer with past papers on top before walking into your exam. Your final grade is correlated with the number of layers you complete. In other words, the more layers you do the higher grade you will achieve. You should do as many layers as possible without negatively impacting other important commitments and your overall university experience."*

At college, I did up to 6 layers for some subjects. However, at university I usually did only 1 or 2 layers. This was because securing good internships and a graduate position was a higher priority for me than achieving top grades. Spending hours and hours completing extra layers to achieve 85% instead of 75% made no sense. If I had left university with one or two internships at top companies and a 2:1 (60%), I would have been very happy. If I left with a first (70%+) and no brand names on my CV, I would have been disappointed. Thankfully, I managed my time well enough to achieve both.

If your grades have a big influence on your future, for example you want a career in academia or a PHD in the same field of study, then you should do as many layers and push for the highest grades possible.

**Melissa:** *"I'm definitely going to do a Masters in Physics and I want to do it at an American university."*

**Me:** *"In that case, your final degree score matters. You should be looking to complete 2 to 3 layers plus past papers before your exams."*

**Melissa:** *"OK. How should I plan this?"*

**Me:** *"Let's create a layered learning timetable for you. How many subjects are you taking this year and how many exams do you have?"*

**Melissa:** *"8 subjects. 8 exams"*

**Me:** *"Are your modules more coursework or exam based? Give me the breakdown."*

**Melissa:** *"Modules 5 to 8 are mainly coursework. 60% of my final mark in each of these modules are determined by my* *coursework and 40% from the final exam. The remaining modules are 10% coursework and 90% exam."*

**Me:** *"You should cover the exam-focused subjects first but we'll talk about that later. I'll need two more things from you:*

1. *Your exam timetable.*
2. *Total number of A4 pages to cover in each of your learning packs."*

**Melissa:** *"I haven't been able to put together all my learning packs because my lecturers haven't given everything yet – what should I do?"*

**Me:** *"Sometimes course staff like to drip-feed course content over time. You can do 3 things here:*

1. *Tell the staff what you are trying to do and ask them to give you everything in advance.*
2. *Grab the course content and notes from someone in the year above.*
3. *Give an educated guess of the total number of pages."*

**Melissa:** *"How much time should I spend revising?"*

After gathering this information, I asked Melissa to complete the table below showing the total number of pages in each of her learning packs:

| Subject | Total No. Pages in Learning Pack |
|---|---|
| 1 | 280 |
| 2 | 183 |
| 3 | 341 |
| 4 | 254 |
| 5 | 231 |
| 6 | 221 |
| 7 | 309 |
| 8 | 242 |

Your layered learning timetable will largely depend on how quickly you can work through the content. Using my study techniques, students average about 6 A4 pages an hour during their first layer. We can use this figure to estimate how long it will take Melissa to learn her subjects.

| Subject | Total No. Pages in Learning Pack | First Layer - No. Hours of Learning |
|---|---|---|
| 1 | 280 | 47 |
| 2 | 183 | 31 |
| 3 | 341 | 57 |
| 4 | 254 | 42 |
| 5 | 231 | 39 |
| 6 | 221 | 37 |
| 7 | 309 | 52 |
| 8 | 242 | 40 |

Melissa will need to spend around 43 hours per subject and allocate a total of 345 hours of self-study to complete her entire first layer. She should work faster through modules 5-8 because the exam only counts for 40% of her grade. However, we can account for this by adjusting her timetable. At this stage, we can use these figures as a guide to determine when she should start preparing.

**Melissa:** *"345 hours - that's a lot of time! How am I going to complete all my coursework and fit all this extra revision in?"*

**Me:** *"You have more free time at university than you did at college. Without teachers breathing down your neck, it can be difficult to manage your time but once you get the hang of it, spending 10-15 hours a week on your first layer is very doable."*

The first layer is the most important one of all. It also takes the longest to complete because it's the first time you're learning the material outside of lectures. So, if you find yourself spending 20-30 minutes on one page of your textbook, don't worry! That's normal and you shouldn't rush.

Moving through the content too quickly is the most common mistake I see students make with their first layers. If you cover 200 pages of your learning pack in a few days, alarm bells should start ringing. This usually indicates that you are not using the correct study technique (described in Chapter 13) and skipping over difficult bits. This is the layer where it's acceptable to make mistakes and be a little stubborn when it comes to understanding tricky concepts. To avoid rushing, within each topic, ask yourself "do I really understand this?" If not, break it down and take your time.

**Melissa:** *"What about the second layer?"*

If you completed your first layer thoroughly using my study techniques before the exam, you are well on your way to achieving a top grade. Going over your learning packs a second time will reaffirm the information and boost your grade further. You should also complete the majority of your past papers during this time. I usually complete all but 3 of the most recent past papers at this point.

As you've already covered the material once before, completing the second layer will be much easier and quicker. Information that you covered weeks ago and thought was forgotten will come rushing back. On average, people hit 10 pages an hour, but 12-14 pages an hour is common. I hit 15 pages an hour for some subjects that I enjoyed. For Melissa's timetable, I used the average rate to calculate how many hours she needs to finish the 2nd layer.

| **Subject** | **Total No. Pages in Learning Pack** | **1st Layer - No. Hours of Learning** | **2nd Layer - No. Hours of Learning** |
|---|---|---|---|
| 1 | 280 | 47 | 28 |
| 2 | 183 | 31 | 18 |
| 3 | 341 | 57 | 34 |
| 4 | 254 | 42 | 25 |
| 5 | 231 | 39 | 23 |
| 6 | 221 | 37 | 22 |
| 7 | 309 | 52 | 31 |
| 8 | 242 | 40 | 24 |

Melissa will need to spend around 26 hours per subject and allocate a total of 205 hours of self-study time to complete her entire second layer.

**Melissa:** *"Eeeeek!"*

**Me:** *"Don't worry! It will be April by the time you get to the 2nd layer and the pressure will be on for exams. Most of your coursework will be finished so you can focus completely on exam preparation."*

**Melissa:** *"Will there be enough time for a third layer?"*

With layer two done, the third layer should be completed in the run up to exams, and in the gaps between exams, alongside past papers (these take priority). You should be skim-reading through your learning packs and jogging your memory. Don't waste any time learning any new content as you are better off reaffirming content you already know. Prioritise subjects that are heavily weighted towards exams by spending more time covering the material in this third layer and by completing a fourth layer.

Four of Melissa's subjects were heavily weighted towards coursework. For those, she could skim read them at 20-30 pages an hour. If you are strapped for time or have performed well in your coursework, you can skip the third layer altogether and just finish the past papers. For the subjects heavily weighted towards exams, move through your packs at a slower rate of 15-20 pages an hour. Melissa had performed quite well in her coursework, so she just needed to skim over the subject over a few hours and complete the last remaining past papers.

| Subject | Total No. Pages in Learning Pack | 1st Layer - No. Hours of Learning | 2nd Layer - No. Hours of Learning | 3rd Layer - No. Hours of Learning |
|---|---|---|---|---|
| 1 | 280 | 47 | 28 | 19 |
| 2 | 183 | 31 | 18 | 12 |
| 3 | 341 | 57 | 34 | 23 |
| 4 | 254 | 42 | 25 | 17 |
| 5 | 231 | 39 | 23 | 7 |
| 6 | 221 | 37 | 22 | 7 |
| 7 | 309 | 52 | 31 | 10 |
| 8 | 242 | 40 | 24 | 7 |

Melissa will need an estimated 621 hours to complete her layered learning timetable and walk into her exams with confidence.

**Melissa:** *"This sounds like a lot of time!"*

**Me:** *"It does, but when the work is spread over several months, it becomes easier to comprehend."*

**Melissa:** *"When should I start preparing for exams?"*

**Me:** *"It depends on how much time you can allocate to self-study each week. Most people start their first layer in January and can spare on average 19 hours a week because of coursework and other commitments. As you approach April and May, you will have less coursework and more time. This is a good time to start your second layer and most students can average 40 hours a week. Your third layer will be completed during the high pressure weeks running into exams – 50+ hours a week is achievable."*

**Melissa:** *"I think April and May will be fine, but I really don't know if I can fit in 19 hours a week in addition to my coursework."*

**Me:** *"It will be challenging but you can do it. At university, there are so many gaps in the day where you can sneak off to a coffee shop or library and fit in an hour or two of work. Even on the busiest weeks I was able to fit in 20 odd hours by working around my coursework and lectures. For example, if we had a lecture on Transport Processes and were given some work, I'd take a crack at the work then learn the whole topic using my study techniques. 1 extra hour of work; Layer 1 on that topic done."*

Based on these proxies and Melissa's schedule, we can calculate how many weeks she will need to complete each layer.

| | **Total hours of work required** | **Hours of self-study per week** | **Total weeks** |
|---|---|---|---|
| **Layer 1** | 345 | 19 | 18 |
| **Layer 2** | 205 | 40 | 5 |
| **Layer 3** | 71 | 50 | 1 |

Working backwards from Melissa's first exam, which is on 1st May, she will need to start preparing in December. If her exams started towards the end of May or beginning of June, she could get away with starting closer to January. Based on this start date and work rate I created Melissa's layered learning timetable.

**Layer 1**

| **Subject** | **Start Date** | **End Date** | **No. of Days** |
|---|---|---|---|
| Module 1 | 1st December | 18th December | 18 |
| Module 2 | 19th December | 5th January | 18 |
| Module 3 | 6th January | 23rd January | 18 |
| Module 4 | 24th January | 10th February | 18 |
| Module 5 | 11th February | 20th February | 10 |
| Module 6 | 21st February | 2nd March | 10 |
| Module 7 | 3rd March | 12th March | 10 |
| Module 8 | 13th March | 22nd March | 10 |

**Layer 2**

| **Subject** | **Start Date** | **End Date** | **No. of Days** |
|---|---|---|---|
| Module 1 | 23rd March | 28th March | 6 |
| Module 2 | 29th March | 3rd April | 6 |
| Module 3 | 4th April | 9th April | 6 |
| Module 4 | 10th April | 15th April | 6 |
| Module 5 | 16th April | 17th April | 2 |
| Module 6 | 18th April | 19th April | 2 |
| Module 7 | 20th April | 21st April | 2 |
| Module 8 | 22nd April | 23rd April | 2 |

L2 = Layer 2
L3 = Layer 3

| | | | | | | |
|---|---|---|---|---|---|---|
| 20<br>Mod 7: L2 | 21<br>Mod 7: L2 | 22<br>Mod 8: L2 | 23<br>Mod 8: L2 | 24<br>Mod 1: L3 | 25<br>Mod 1: L3 | 26<br>Mod 2: L3 |
| 27<br>Mod 2: L3 | 28<br>Mod 3: L3 | 29<br>Mod 6: L3 | 30<br>Mod 6: L3 | **May 1**<br>**Mod 6: Exam** | 2<br>Mod 3: L3 | 3<br>Mod 3: L3 |

| | | | | | | |
|---|---|---|---|---|---|---|
| 4<br>Mod 2: L3 | 5<br>Mod 2: L3<br>Mod 3: L4 | 6<br>**Mod 2: Exam**<br>**Mod 3: Exam**<br>Mod 1: L4 | 7<br>**Mod 1: Exam**<br>Mod 8: L3 | 8<br>Mod 8: L3 | 9<br>Mod 8: L3 | 10<br>Mod 8: L3 |
| 11<br>Mod 8: L3 | 12<br>Mod 8: L3 | 13<br>Mod 8: L3 | 14<br>Mod 8: L3 | 15<br>**Mod 8: Exam** | 16<br>Mod 5: L3 | 17<br>Mod 5: L3 |
| 18<br>Mod 5: L3 | 19<br>Mod 5: L3 | 20<br>**Mod 5: Exam** | 21<br>Mod 4: L3 | 22<br>Mod 4: L3 | 23<br>Mod 4: L3 | 24<br>Mod 4: L3 |
| 25<br>Mod 4: L3 | 26<br>Mod 4: L3 | 27<br>Mod 4: L3 | 28<br>Mod 4: L3 | 29<br>**Mod 4: Exam** | 30<br>Mod 7: L3 | 31<br>Mod 7: L3 |

| | | | | | | |
|---|---|---|---|---|---|---|
| **June 1**<br>Mod 7: L3 | 2<br>Mod 7: L3 | 3<br>**Mod 7: Exam** | 4<br>☺ | 5 | 6 | 7 |

**Melissa:** *"Do I really need to start revising for my June exams over the Christmas holidays?"*

**Me:** *"It would be a safe bet. If you can work through the content at 8-10 pages an hour or fit in 30-40 hours of revision per week starting from January, by all means start in January. But if I was in your position, I would start a little earlier."*

**Melissa:** *"Would I have to revise 1 module at a time, or can I revise several on the go?"*

**Me:** *"I prefer to revise one subject at a time, but you can work on several different subjects at the same time. For example, you could work on Mod 1 on Monday, Mod 2 on Tuesday and Mod 3 on Wednesday. No matter how you decide to do it, at least 2 layers and all past papers need to be completed before walking into your exam. Use the timetable as a guide to keep you on track rather than a fixed schedule."*

**Melissa:** *"Why have you allocated more days for modules 1-4?"*

**Me:** *"The exams for these modules account for 90% of your grade so you should dedicate more time and work through them in greater detail."*

**Melissa:** *"With some exams, you have shown that I need to complete a fourth layer and some you haven't. Why is this?"*

During your exam period, be wary of 'exam clusters' where there are several exams in a short space of time or across consecutive days.

Take a look at the first two weeks of Melissa's exam timetable:

| 20 | 21 | 22 | 23 | 24 | 25 | 26 |
|---|---|---|---|---|---|---|
| Mod 7: L2 | Mod 7: L2 | Mod 8: L2 | Mod 8: L2 | Mod 1: L3 | Mod 1: L3 | Mod 2: L3 |
| **27** | **28** | **29** | **30** | **May 1** | **2** | **3** |
| Mod 2: L3 | Mod 3: L3 | Mod 6: L3 | Mod 6: L3 | **Mod 6: Exam** | Mod 3: L3 | Mod 3: L3 |

| 4 | 5 | 6 | 7 | 8 | 9 | 10 |
|---|---|---|---|---|---|---|
| Mod 2: L3 | Mod 2: L3<br>Mod 3: L4 | **Mod 2: Exam**<br>**Mod 3: Exam**<br>Mod 1: L4 | **Mod 1: Exam**<br>Mod 8: L3 | Mod 8: L3 | Mod 8: L3 | Mod 8: L3 |

May 6th and 7th is an exam cluster where she has 3 exams across 2 days. To prepare for these exams in the middle of clusters, it's important that you complete the third layer for the last exam in advance. For example, Melissa should revise module 1 before 2 and 3.

To sufficiently prepare for the exams in the middle or end of the cluster (Module 3 and 1 in Melissa's case), complete a quick 4th layer and work through past papers on the night before or the morning of the exam. This extra layer will compensate for the lack of time you have before the exam.

**It's OK to Become Obsessed with Doing Layers!**

Revising using layers can make you quite an obsessive person. You will constantly feel paranoid about forgetting information and have the urge to squeeze in more layers. I used to randomly test myself and whenever I forgot a small piece of information, I would become extremely paranoid: Was this just the tip of the iceberg? How many other pieces of information have I forgotten?

Having this paranoia pushed me to complete more layers, especially during the gaps between exams. At college, on some difficult topics, I would complete up to six layers just out of fear that I'd forgotten everything. After six layers, there was no forgetting anything in those topics. I could have drawn out every damn picture on each page if you asked me to. The point is – paranoia is good. Embrace it!

## Track your Progress

Check your progress continuously week by week and day by day, especially towards the tail end of the year when you start preparing for your exams. Once you've set your layered learning timetable and finalised your learning packs, calculate how many pages you need to cover per week.

Take a look at Melissa's first 3 modules:

**Layer 1**

| **Subject** | **Start Date** | **End Date** | **No. of Days** | **Pages in Learning Pack** | **Pages per week** | **Pages per day** |
|---|---|---|---|---|---|---|
| Mod 1 | 1st Dec | 18th Dec | 18 | 280 | **108** | **15.5** |
| Mod 2 | 19th Dec | 5th Jan | 18 | 183 | **71** | **10** |
| Mod 3 | 6th Jan | 23rd Jan | 18 | 341 | **133** | **19** |

For her first module, she will need to complete around 15 pages a day and 108 pages a week to complete her first layer on time. This amounts to 2-3 hours of work a day.

## When to Revise?

- Learning the same information multiple times helps you memorise information for longer.

- The layered learning timetable should be completed in addition to other work set by your course staff.

## When to Study?

- You can cover all your subjects one at a time or all at once 'in tune' with your course schedule.

- Squeeze in a fourth layer if you have time, particularly during exam clusters.

- Track your progress by checking how many pages you are completing each week and per day.

- You should complete at least one layer and all the past papers for each subject or module before walking into your exams.

You now know how to put together your learning packs, what to revise and when to revise using the layered learning approach. Now it's time to learn how to revise.

**If you're struggling with any of the guidance offered in this section, drop us a message on AcademicUnderdogs.com and we'll be happy to help.**

# Execution – Efficient Learning

# Chapter 13
# **How to Study?**

It's important to have a plan and know when and how to revise for your exams. It helps to maintain order and ensures that you don't miss deadlines or fall behind. However, this is only part of the battle. It makes sense to set goals like the following:

*'I'm going to start revising in January'*

and

*'I'm going to study 19 hours a week'*

But actually committing to those things and following through with them is a differently thing entirely. Managing your time, consistently pushing yourself to work and warding off the swathes of distractions that enter your head is incredibly hard!

All this would be easier if we were interested in our course. However, in reality there will be lots of content that you have zero interest in learning. This doesn't stop after university and you're going to encounter this issue in the workplace too. There will be tasks you intrinsically enjoy and ones you can't wait to finish. Those who can perform well in both tasks are the ones who progress faster. Without sounding too arrogant, this is what I excel at.

## How to Study?

When people ask me to give one core reason why I consistently performed well at college and university, it wouldn't be my ability to plan my revision, choose the correct learning material or network with specialists from the year above. My strength is my ability to learn information quickly and motivate myself to do tasks that I don't want to do.

This learning process hasn't come easy. It has taken years of trial and error, failed exams and heartache to get to this level. Everything I teach you in this section has helped me consistently achieve top grades and beat my peers despite having an average IQ.

**Ready, Aim, Execute!**

Over the next few chapters I'm going to run you through my revision strategy.

1) I'm going to show you how to memorise and learn large volumes of information using the highly efficient 'Scribble Technique'.

2) I'll describe how using this powerful technique and gamifying your overall revision process can boost your marks.

3) In the Motivation section, I'll describe how small changes in your day to day habits can result in big changes to your grades!

# Chapter 14

# How to Learn Large Volumes of Information

International Relations & Business, Medicine, Economics, Architecture, Civil Engineering, Theology and Mandarin – these are all very different subjects with different requirements, but they have something in common. At some point students studying these subjects will have to take one or more exams under timed conditions. To succeed in these exams, regardless of what subject you are taking you'll need to commit large volumes of information to memory.

Studying German? Before answering any exam questions for these subjects, you'll need to memorise all the verbs and adjectives. Taking Engineering? There will be a bunch of formulas and mathematical proofs you'll need to memorise. Regardless of how good your other skills are, if the required information is not in your head on exam day, you'll struggle to achieve top marks. Memory and learning techniques are everything!

**Me:** *"Right – You've finished your day's lectures and have returned to your room. The learning pack for the first module you want to revise is sitting on your desk. What do you do?"*

**Melissa:** *"Just start reading and learning it."*

**Me:** *"How will you learn it? Let's be specific."*

**Melissa:** *"I guess I'll start with the handouts and create notes based on what I read."*

**Me:** *"What will you do with those notes?"*

**Melissa:** *"Make sure they are neat and filed for me to read through later."*

**Me:** *"Can you show me an example of notes you've taken in the past?"*

### Note Taking and Summarising, is it Worth it?

Melissa took some of the most beautifully written, multi-coloured and Instagram-worthy notes I have ever seen. But I couldn't help but sigh when she gave me her notes, just like I had done with so much students before her. I used to believe that highlighting and summarising key information was a good learning method. I also thought that reading my notes closer to the exam would then the deal. Unfortunately, I was wrong. Here's why this method is nowhere near as effective as many students believe:

### 1. Missing Information and Important Details

Summarising the course content into your own personal notes is a dangerous game to play, especially if you plan on using those notes to revise. Given that your lecturers could test you on practically anything from the course syllabus, how do you choose what to note down and what to leave out?

Let's imagine that your learning pack contains close to 100% of what you need to know. By summarising and cherry-picking information that *you* felt was important, your notes would undoubtedly contain a fraction of the information in your learning pack and therefore a fraction of the information required for your exam.

For the sake of this example, let's assume this fraction is 70%.

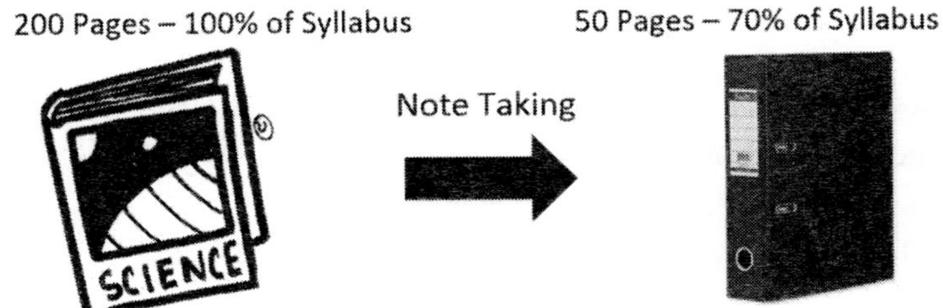


If you then use your summarised notes to revise, it will be difficult to retain more than 80% of the information in your notes. For argument sake, let's assume you store 80% of the information from your notes in your memory. This means on exam-day, your brain will contain 56% of the required course content (80% of 70% = 56%).

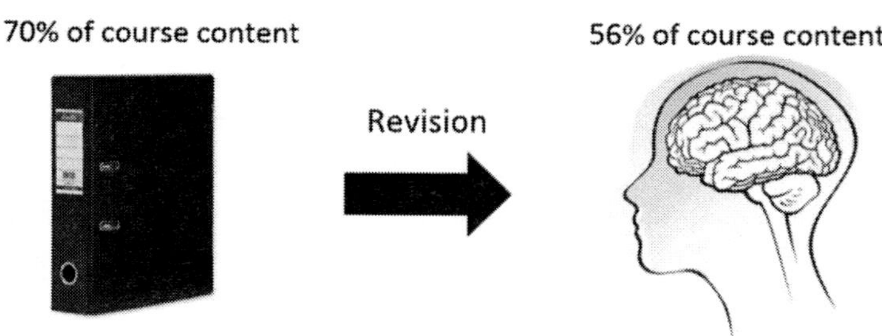


Coupled with the pressure and nervous on the day, walking into the exam with only 56% of the required information does not give you a good chance of achieving a top grade.

**2. Temptation to Procrastinate and Waste Time**

Students spend unreasonable amounts of money on simple stationery. They buy multi-coloured pens and notebooks and they waste hours jotting down information they deem to be useful. Why do all of this when you can simply read existing educational material?

I admit that note taking, if done properly, can make it easier to revise from your own notes, but is it worth spending all that extra time compiling those notes?

**3. Fool's Gold**

When taking notes, it's easy to fool yourself into thinking you've done a lot of work when you haven't actually done much at all. I've met many students who feel that copying from a textbook is a great way to learn and a valid way of completing a layer. I'm sorry to say, this is simply not true.

Don't get caught in the trap of studying just so that you can say that you did x hours of work today to make yourself feel good. Ask yourself what you have learned. It's better to do one hour of revision and take 2 things in, rather than 5 hours and take in nothing! Passive note taking is like writing on a typewriter without the keys making contact with the page – lots of effort and time spent but nothing retained.

If you've put together your learning packs correctly, this is all that's required and there's no need to do any summarising or bullet pointing. Learning directly from these packs can help you achieve a 2:1, first, pass, merit or whatever you're aiming for.

**Melissa:** *"What if I re-word the information in textbooks and handouts in my own words?"*

**Me:** *"It would be a better approach than just highlighting and copying. However, you'll still end up cherry-picking all the important information."*

**Melissa:** *"I have to admit – this does make sense. So, if I shouldn't take notes, what should I do instead?"*

**Me:** *"You should learn directly from your learning material using one core learning method which you can use again and* *again to prepare for your exams. I recommend using The Scribble Technique®."*

**The Scribble Technique®**

This technique is a powerful memory tool that I've used time and time again. I attribute most of my exam success, particularly with subjects that required a lot of fact learning, to this simple 8-step process:

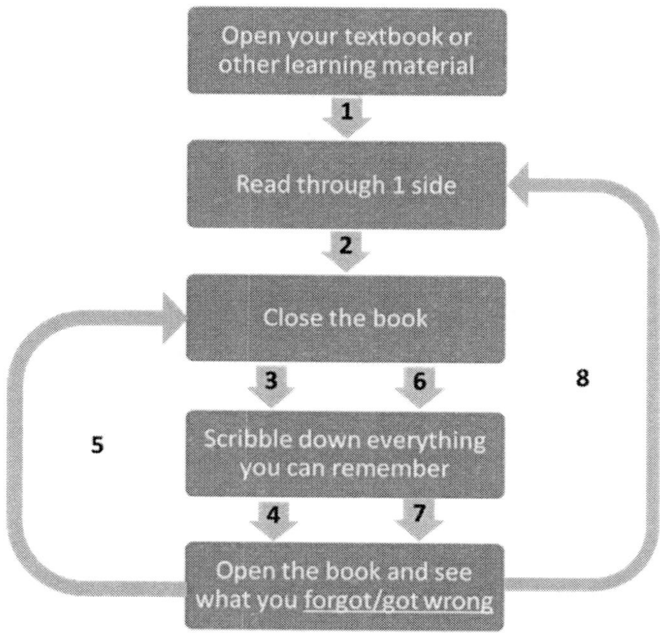

**Scribble Technique vs. Note Taking: Which is Better?**

The Scribble Technique on its own is a very effective way of absorbing and retaining information. It's also a faster way of learning large volumes of information. The high efficiency and effectiveness of this technique makes it easier to bypass any note taking and focus on learning material there and then. Using this technique for each layer can help you retain 80%, if not more, of the information in your learning pack.

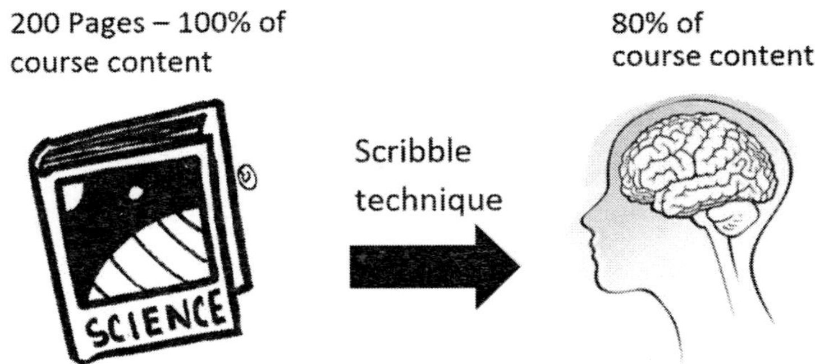


Focusing on memorising and learning the material, means you'll be happy to make mistakes and forget things when scribbling because you will open the page again and see what you missed or got wrong. The constant process of making mistakes and correcting them helps you retain information in a much faster and superior way to standard note taking.

Have you ever heard a song on the radio which you liked the sound of, but when you returned home to search for it on Youtube you forgot the name? It's on the tip of your tongue but you just can't get hold of it. You keep trying to remember and wait, wait some more… then …POP! The name appears out of nowhere and you experience that brief pointless moment of joy! Chances are that song name will be stuck in your memory from that point onwards.

Effective memory retention is all about creating those pointless moments of joy after challenging yourself to remember something. It might sound silly, but the more 'pops' you can produce the more you will remember.

**Gamify your Learning Process**

During A-Levels, I was so angry at myself for failing that I started working like a mad man. I had over 20 exams to sit in June, so I set very ambitious daily study targets. For Biology, I made a commitment to learn 30 pages a day over the last few weeks of the summer holiday. This was crazy because during first year I could barely complete 30 pages in a week let alone a day. To hit these targets, I needed to work several hours a day. This required an incredible amount of stamina and an abnormal attention span!

In an attempt to meet these targets, after trying a few study techniques, I settled on using the Scribble Technique® for no other reason than 'it felt right'. Only after I beat the clever kids in my class and scored 90%+ in my Biology re-takes did I begin wondering why it was so effective. After a few months of using this approach, I was working harder than I had ever done in my life and my attention span had almost tripled (I timed it with a stopwatch). Then it dawned on me! This process of learning felt more like a game than it did a revision technique.

**Scribble Technique® vs Angry Birds**

Candy Crush, Angry Birds, Tetris, Pacman, Flappy Bird – these are all ridiculously simple games that keep people entertained for hours. With Angry Birds, you throw a bird into a pile of stuff with a view to knocking it over. It has been downloaded over 3 billion times. If people can be addicted to simple repetitive games like this, is it really a stretch to assume we can become mildly addicted to other repetitive tasks like revision?

Engaging games like Angry Birds have tasks that seem simple on the surface but can be quite challenging. Have you ever tried those games at carnivals and theme parks? Like the one where you knock down a set of seemingly flimsy cups with a heavy ball from a few meters? Even after you've tried it multiple times it *still* looks easy. There's this inner voice that keeps telling you, "I should be able to do this!" Then, after finally mastering it, you lose interest. This is why game designers add levels to keep players engaged. They also offer rewards that provide instant gratification. Carnival games, for example, offer toys as a reward.

For me, the Scribble Technique turned from a revision technique into a memory game. It wasn't as engaging or addictive as Fortnite, COD or any other professionally designed game. However, it had just enough characteristics of a game to keep me engaged for long periods of time even when I had no interest in what I was learning.

Every time I turned a page in my learning material, my goal was to remember every single piece of information without peeking. From first glance, this seemed simple but no matter how much I tried, I always forgot some key fact or important point. This bugged me! Every time I remembered a difficult fact or a complicated concept, I got a small dopamine hit and dose of satisfaction. The elusiveness of remembering everything on each page and the instant gratification of remembering some parts kept me going. After a few weeks of using this approach, something amazing happened; I started developing a genuine interest in my subjects!

**Chicken or the Egg?**

**Melissa:** *"I'm definitely going to fail Module 4 – I have no interest in it whatsoever and my lecturer's voice is more monotonous than the white-noise my sister uses to send my niece to sleep."*

**Me:** *"Have you tried to get stuck into the course on your own?"*

**Melissa:** *"How do I motivate myself to learn the content if I have zero interest in it?"*

**Me:** *"How do you become interested if you don't try and learn the content?"*

This is a classic Chicken and Egg scenario that I hear all the time. You have to go with the Chicken and use every trick, hack or game to motivate yourself to work through the content first, then allow your interest to develop later.

After completing my first layer in A-level Biology using the Scribble Technique, I started uncontrollably daydreaming about what I had learnt. A mother and baby walked past me on the street and I thought of Meiosis. I spotted a massive tree while staring out of a bus window - photosynthesis. My friend's dog bit my jeans – positive and negative reinforcement in animals. I developed a genuine interest in my subjects only after a sustained effort to learn the subject. Gamifying your revision process and then continuously trying to get better at the game will help you achieve this.

## Understand, don't Memorise

When using the Scribble Technique® it wasn't long before I realised that to consistently achieve a 'high score' I couldn't just memorise everything word for word. I had to ***understand*** what was on each page. This is when I tried all sorts of looney psychological experiments and ideas to help me. For example, when learning how DNA molecules replicate, I closed my eyes and vividly imagined the enzyme Helicase going over to the molecule and unzipping the double helix.

I would make my visualisations as vivid as possible almost as if I was watching it in real life. I'd also make them crazy and dramatic. For example, I'd imagine the Helicase molecule taking a baseball bat and beating the crap out of the DNA molecule until it split in two. If anyone read my mind while I was using the Scribble Technique, they would probably recommend professional help! But, using these tricks, I was able to understand complex information to the point I could explain it back to myself or someone else. I'll describe some of the other tricks and hacks I used in the Motivation section.

## How to Learn Large Volumes of Information

Notice how there are no coloured pencils, highlighters or flash cards mentioned in this chapter. My learning approach is very industrial; designed to get you to the table and stay there long enough to learn everything you need.

Having made it to university, you probably have your own learning processes that have helped you so far. If you haven't achieved top grades in your pre-university exams, I suggest using the Scribble Technique® for at least 3 weeks. It won't take you long to realise why I rate it so much.

Your attention span and focus will improve. Once you are immersed in the overall learning process, all those annoying, distracting, negative insecure voices in your head will turn into whispers. If you focus on perfecting each page, then achieving top grades will almost become incidental.

Each year, I receive hundreds of e-mails from students who have improved their grades using the Scribble Technique® or other gamified learning processes.

- Learn directly from your learning packs using the Scribble Technique® (ST) instead of making summarised notes.
- When using the ST, don't peek after you close the book.
- Stubbornly challenge yourself to remember as much as you can.
- Aim to get better at the game every day.

It won't be long before this process of learning becomes engaging and maybe even slightly addictive.

# Chapter 15
# **Bag of Tricks**

**Melissa:** *"Apart from the Scribble Technique, is there anything else you used?"*

**Me:** *"Very occasionally I used alternative memory techniques like 'picture association' and mnemonics to memorise very arduous pieces of information. Mind maps were also a very useful tool."*

### Mind Mapping – Mental Filing System

It's very easy to become so bogged down in detail that you struggle to recall the correct information or become mixed up with other material you have learnt.

Practicing past papers helps, but you also need to have an organised thought process to avoid confusing yourself during your exams. If you've focused on the details too much during your layers, the organisation of that information in your mind will be poor. Let me give you an example:

In maths, there are many methods that are similar; without proper mind mapping you can accidently use one method when you're supposed to use another. Integration and differentiation (from maths) is an example of such a scenario. These methods are used in calculus and using one instead of the other can result in completely the wrong answer.

Most people, including myself, create these mental mind-maps naturally while revising. However, I've come across some students who don't. Usually, if a student with strong motivation and good revision technique underachieves, it's because of poor mind mapping.

**Good vs. Poor Mind Mapping**

The best way to gauge your mind mapping skills is to analyse how you link any given exam/practice question to the information required to answer it (in your memory bank). The diagrams below show the thought processes of a good and poor mind mapper:

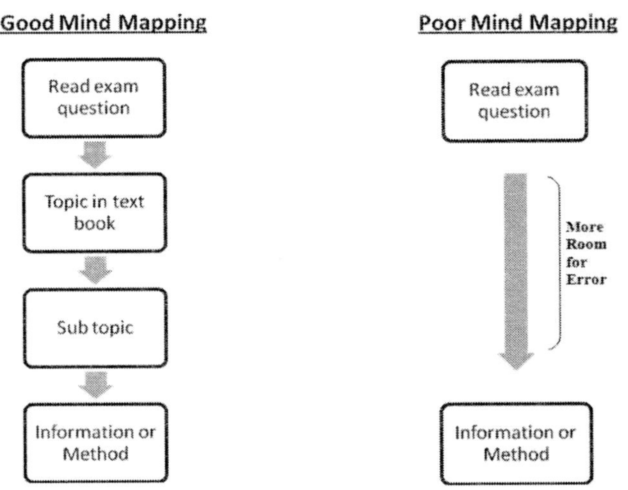

As you can see, a good mind mapper not only learns the information or method, but also has an idea of what topic or chapter it falls under. Therefore, the topics are categorised, and you can create clear dividing lines. This leaves less room for error and prevents confusion.

**Are you a Natural Mind Mapper?**

If you can bring up topic/chapter names during general conversation, then you'll probably be good at mind mapping. For example, a Psychology student discussing a module with his/her friends would probably ask questions like, 'Is that from chapter 4?' or 'didn't we cover that during the Cognitive Psychology lecture a few weeks back?' You can always tell when someone doesn't mind map because when you mention the names of certain topics or chapter headings, they have a blank look on their face.

**If you don't naturally mind map, what can you do?**

After the first layer of a subject, I could usually think of a piece of information, open my textbook and pick out the chapter it was in. In some cases, I can remember the actual page. It isn't as difficult as it sounds if you adopt certain habits during your study cycle, such as regularly reviewing material, reaffirming topics and physical mind mapping.

## Regularly Reviewing Previous Material

Every time you finish a study session, briefly go over the information you have covered, summarise it into a few lines and remind yourself of the topic and/or subtopic it falls under. Repeat this on a day-to-day basis before starting a new self-study session. It shouldn't take more than a couple of minutes.

## Reaffirming Topics

Be the person who knows all the names to the chapters and topics. Talk about the chapters out loud when discussing with friends or tutors to reaffirm them. When your professor brings up a topic during a lecture, think about the summaries you have made during self-study.

This helps to cement the topics in your memory. It's a similar story with dream journals. If you want to remember your dreams, the best thing to do is write them down upon waking or talk about them with someone. You won't necessarily need to review your text or conversation at a later date, as it's the act of committing to writing/speaking that cements those dreams in your memory.

When trying to remember key parts of a text, writing them down, talking about them or speaking them out loud will often be enough for you to remember them.

## Physical Mind Mapping

Physically drawing mind maps can be very beneficial. If you haven't come across them before, here's an example of one for Physics.

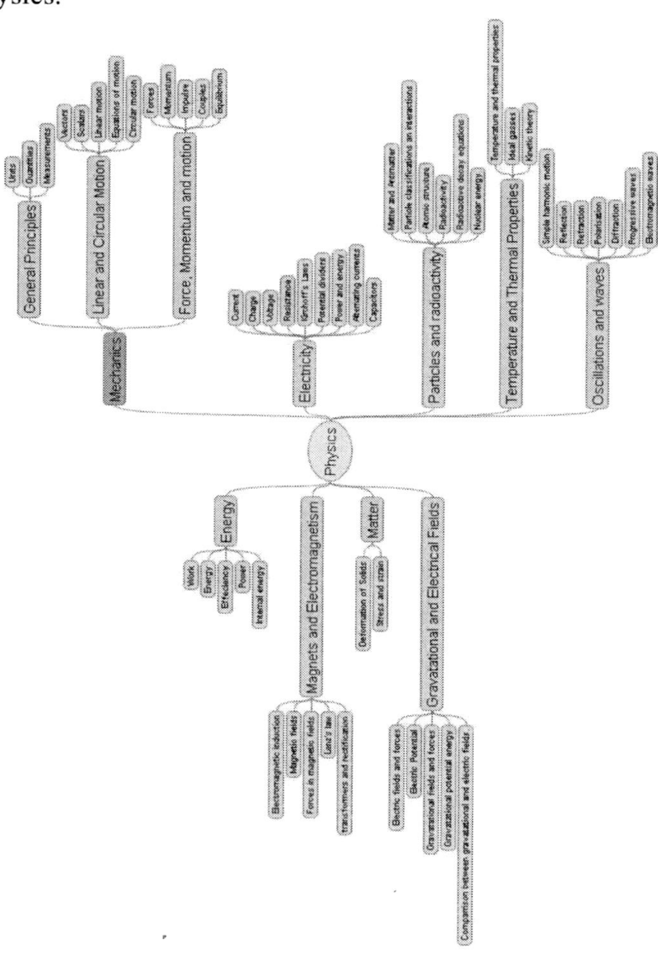

Before the actual exam use the mind map as a guide and run through the topics and summarisations you've made.

**Mind Mapping Tutorial**

There are also some apps and websites that can help you build mind maps. However, I recommend doing it the old-fashioned way and drawing them out on an A4 or A3 piece of paper.

**Step 1:** Write your subject name at the centre of the page.

**Step 2:** Use the bullet points in your course synopsis or syllabus to choose the labels for the first layer of branches.

**Step 3:** Draw branches to key topics that fall under each bullet point.

Given that we want the mind map to show an overview of a subject or module, I wouldn't produce any further branches. As you read over your mind map think/write about the important details that fall under each topic.

I never created an actual mind map. However, by thoroughly reviewing modules and completing multiple layers on chapters/topics, I naturally made my own mental filing system. If you find that you are unable to do this, you must make a conscious effort to do so. Take time out from your study cycle and physically create mind maps.

At university, information from different subjects often overlaps. Effective mind mapping will save a significant amount of time.

**Bag of Tricks: Alternative Memory Techniques**

For some exam questions, you may have to memorise information in the form of an item list or process. For example, in biology, transcription is a process whereby a protein molecule is built in a cell. This process has 6 steps which students will need to remember for the exam. Typically, layered learning and the Scribble Technique® are powerful enough to commit this information to memory, however, it doesn't hurt to have a few more tricks up your sleeve. This makes sure you remember all you need in the exam.

Our minds can only remember a limited number of items at a time. Even after layers, some information is awkward and arduous to memorise. Picture association and mnemonics are useful aids for these scenarios, so let's have a look at these now.

**Picture Association**

This technique involves creating memory triggers by first associating objects with numbers and then the objects with information we want to learn. Our minds find it easier to remember objects and scenarios as opposed to numbers or facts. Therefore, we can use an object to create a mental link between the items of information we want to learn and the corresponding item number.

This technique is not only useful for an item list which must be remembered in a consecutive order, but also if you need to call upon a specific item or number.

For example, earlier I mentioned the transcription process most biology students need to learn. In step 2 of the transcription process, an enzyme called RNA polymerase unwinds and unlinks the two strands of DNA. In the exam, you may have to recall this specific step or know where this step occurs in the process. With picture association, you can easily remember the object associated with the step number and therefore remember the information associated with the object.

***Picture Association Tutorial:***

**Step 1**: Assign memorable objects to numbers 1 – 15. Use the ones we have here.

| Number | Object | Reason |
|---|---|---|
| 1 | Tree | 1 tree stands alone |
| 2 | Light Switch | 2 options: on and off |
| 3 | Traffic Light | 3 options: green, amber and red |
| 4 | Dog | A dog has 4 legs |
| 5 | Glove | A glove has 5 fingers |
| 6 | Devil | The devil's number is 666 |
| 7 | Heaven | 7 rhymes with heaven |
| 8 | Skate | 8 rhymes with skate |
| 9 | Cat | A cat has 9 lives |
| 10 | Bowling Ball | 10 pin bowling |
| 11 | Twin Towers | September 11th attacks and the twin towers looked like 11 |
| 12 | Eggs | 12 Dozen in a pack of eggs |
| 13 | Pumpkin | 13 is "unlucky" – Halloween – pumpkin |
| 14 | Flowers | 14th Feb is Valentine's day where you give/receive flowers |
| 15 | Cinema Ticket | Only over 15's allowed for some cinema movies |

Once you have memorised and associated each number to an object, these objects become **Number Associated Objects**.

This means the number and object are interchangeable – whenever you think of the number 2 you should almost immediately think 'light switch' and vice versa.

Task

1. Memorise and scribble down the number, association and object down three times:

...

"2...On & Off...Light Switch"

"3.....Red, Amber & Green....Traffic Light"

...

2. Then do it backwards three times:

...

"Light Switch...On & Off...2"

"Traffic Light...Red, Amber and Green...3"

**Step 2**: Use your imagination to link the **Number Associated Object** to the item of information. You do this by imagining a memorable scenario.

For example, for step 2 in the transcription process, we can imagine the RNA polymerase approaching the DNA strand and pressing a light switch which then causes the DNA to unwind.

This method might sound silly but that's exactly why it will stick in your head. It's easier for your mind to remember scenarios than sentences/numbers and it's even easier if those scenarios are funny or crazy. When imagining the scenario, close your eyes and make it vivid and clear.

**Mnemonic**

This is a common technique backed by many studies, used to help retain and recall information. In this section, we will look at the two most effective types of mnemonics: music and expression/word.

## Music

Can you recite a song's lyrics after only hearing it a handful of times? Some people can, but the vast majority, myself included, cannot. If you can, it's probably because the fundamental systems in your mind are highly sensitive to melody and rhyme. This can be useful for remembering information.

When you think about music mnemonics you probably picture the 'ABC' song used to help primary school kids learn the alphabet. However, although useful, this is not the technique I am referring to. Instead of creating song lyrics out of information, a more efficient way to use your 'musical mind' is to use songs in conjunction with the Scribble Technique. This can be done by reading (out loud or in your mind) information from your textbook in a musical way. You can then benefit by combining the highly efficient forgetting-remembering cycle in the Scribble Technique with the mental links created using your unique 'musical mind'.

## Expression or Word

Using expression or word mnemonics is also a useful memory technique. When memorising a list of items, you can produce a word mnemonic using the first letter of each item of information.

For example, in English, to join two clauses together you use coordinating conjunctions. These are: for, and, nor, but, or, yet and so. These can be remembered using the word mnemonic FANBOYS.

An expression mnemonic can also be used:

| For | And | Nor | But | Or | Yet | So |
|---|---|---|---|---|---|---|
| Four | Apples | Nearly | Broke | On | Your | Sidewalk |

If you don't want to spend time thinking of mnemonics like these then you can find existing ones online or by using mnemonic calculators.

In comparison to the Scribble Technique, both these techniques are less efficient. Therefore, I would only use them for memorising a multi-step sequence or for information that you are struggling to retain even after several layers. Please do not replace the Scribble Technique with these alternative memory tricks – you will run out of time!

# Chapter 16
# Past Papers

There isn't a lot that can be said about past papers, but they still need to be covered as they are pivotal to your success. Studies done by several education companies, mine included, have found a strong correlation between past papers completed and exam marks. This relationship exists during high school and college, but past papers become even more important during university.

Your department doesn't have the same resources as a large exam board like Edexcel. Therefore, they don't have time to develop new past papers each year. As a result, universities tend to recycle questions from previous exam papers and change them slightly. Not all departments do this, but most of the students we've polled across the UK have seen this trend.

Your course department may only release a limited quantity of past papers because they may want to reuse questions from older papers. **Go to your main university library and ask for archived past papers.** If that doesn't work, message every single alumnus on LinkedIn and Facebook until you find these archived papers.

After you have all the papers, find topics or questions that are repeated two or more times and learn how to answer them. If variations of these questions appear in your exam, you can lock these marks down quickly and give yourself more time to tackle new questions.

## Reducing your Exam Anxiety

As a rule of thumb, your final mark in the exam will be close to the average mark across your last 3 past papers. This is why you should recreate exams conditions on your own and always complete past papers within the specified time limit. Mark yourself harshly and correct what you get wrong. Completing your past papers this way will reduce your anxiety.

Some level of anxiety is healthy, but most of the time it has a negative effect. Our minds don't work at full capacity when placed under great emotional stress. In the days running up to exams, there will be a bunch of, 'What if?' questions running through your mind. One of my anxieties was, 'What if I don't finish on time?'

The uncertainty around exams will drive you crazy and prevent you from performing to your best on the day. Completing your past papers in this way will reduce some of this uncertainty because you'll have an idea of what the result will be before it arrives.

## Past Papers

- Find archived past papers from your department, main university library and alumni.

## Past Papers

- Identify topics and questions that appear more than once and ensure you understand how to answer these.

- Complete at least 3 past papers under timed exam conditions.

- **If you run out of time closer to exams, prioritise your past papers over everything else.**

# Chapter 17

# Subject Type and Exam Preparation

Most of your subjects at university can be categorised into 3 groups:

1) **Fact Recall** – The subjects that come under this category generally have large volumes of facts which you'll need to memorise and recall in the exam. Exam questions would usually ask for short answers.

2) **Method and Understanding** – These subjects require understanding, practice and a relatively small amount of fact learning. Exam questions would usually ask for short answers.

3) **Written Prose** – Subjects that require the ability to convert facts and opinions into written prose. Exam questions would usually ask for long answers.

This is how I categorised some of my subjects at university:

## Subject Type and Exam Preparation

| Subject | Fact Recalling | Method & Understanding | Written Prose |
|---|---|---|---|
| Mathematics | | • | |
| Management | | | • |
| Computer Aided Des. | | • | |
| Transport Processes | • | • | |
| Organic Chemistry | • | | |
| Process Heat Transfer | • | • | |
| Chemical Reactions | • | • | |

Each category requires a different approach when it comes to preparing for the final exam. Written prose subjects, such as Management, will require good analysis and essay writing skills; Organic Chemistry needs a lot of fact learning and regurgitation.

As you can see from the table, these categories can overlap. For modules where you have an equal amount of fact-learning and method-understanding, a combination of techniques can be used.

Create your own table at the start of each year. If you aren't sure which categories your subjects fall under, check past papers to see the style and if they contain short (1 – 12 marks) or long essay-based (13+ marks) questions. The section below will explain the optimum methods for each category based on my research and own experience.

### 1) Fact Recall Subjects

From the table, you can see that many of my subjects fall into the 'fact recall' category. These subjects are the easiest ones to achieve top marks in because exam questions rarely ask you to analyse information or to explain your opinion. Also, there is no room for interpretation because the answers are clearly defined by the lecturer's mark scheme – it's black or white. You either remember the facts and get the answer right or you forget them and fall short. The benefit is that you can focus all your efforts on memorising/understanding.

**How to Revise on Your Own?**

If your learning pack covers most of the syllabus, completing 2 or 3 layers using the Scribble Technique is the surest way to achieve 70% or above in your exam.

Two months into my second year of university, one of my lecturers gave me all the handouts for his course. I cross checked these with a friend from the year above and finalised the learning pack. I then finished the first layer using the Scribble Technique for the entire subject. Because of various coursework commitments, it took me just over five weeks to learn 300+ pages. Several months go by – during which time I had a bad break up, several internship assessment centres and a shed load of coursework – and I decided to try a past paper. I fully expected to fail, only to achieve 73%! After completing a second layer and all the remaining past papers a few days before the exam, I improved my final mark to 97%. The

Scribble Technique works very well for 'Fact Recall' subjects and is why I tend to select these subjects when given the opportunity.

**Fact Recall: What to do in Lectures?**

If your textbook and handouts cover everything you need for the exam, don't bother making any notes during class. Just focus on learning and understanding whatever is being taught. Lecturers often drop hints about exams and can give you an insight on 'hot topics' that are likely to come up. Keep post-it notes ready and whenever your lecturer drops a hint, stick one next to the relevant section in your textbook.

Furthermore, always look to learn information during lectures. If there's ever a quiet gap when your professor isn't explaining something, scribble down the key points you remember from the lecture.

Remember that, in addition to doing multiple layers, absorbing information through different channels improves the ability to retain content. These channels are reading, writing, speaking, hearing and doing. By being interactive in lectures you use all these channels at once and therefore improve your chances of remembering key information in the exam.

**2) Method and 'Understanding' Subjects**

Studying maths, sciences or any of the engineering disciplines? Most of your courses will fall under this category.

## How to Revise on your Own

Intelligence and a certain analytical mind can help with these subjects, but this is by no means a prerequisite. Problem solving is engaging and often enjoyable because it inherently shares many characteristics with puzzles or gaming. Each practice question is a puzzle that you need to solve and immersing yourself in that puzzle is relatively easy. Quite often, problems become harder as you progress through the course and this is similar to 'levelling up' in gaming. All these factors, combined with the dopamine hit you get from solving each problem, means 'method and understanding exams' are comparatively less boring and therefore easier to revise for.

For subjects like maths, the general advice that most tutors preach is practice, practice, practice. As a rule of thumb, the more practice questions you complete before the exam, the higher your mark will be – it's as simple as that.

## Textbooks

Most textbooks contain practice questions. However, if you get stuck on a question it's critical that you don't look at the answer too quickly. Be stubborn, allow yourself to feel insulted by the fact you can't figure it out using your head and keep pounding at the question until you're exhausted. It's more beneficial if you come up with an answer and then check if it's right, even if it ultimately proves to be incorrect. I remember occasions when I became extremely stubborn, refused to look at answers and deliberated over single questions for long periods of time.

In a similar way to the Scribble Technique® described earlier, the process of pounding at a question and then having that 'lightbulb moment' will create a strong memory. If that question appears in the exam you'll remember it and will know the answer. The more questions you do and the more stubborn you are with completing them without help, the better chance you'll have of remembering them when they appear.

**Method and Understanding: What to do in Lectures?**

With problem solving, there are always a bunch of tricks and shortcuts which can make your life easier in the exam. Your professors might show you these in lectures, so it would be a good idea to have a few sets of notes outlining all the important hints and tips. What you don't want is pages and pages of classroom notes with different examples explaining the same thing.

### 3) Written Prose Subjects

With 'written prose' exams, simply memorising information prior to your exam won't get you top marks. You need to be able to write essays coherently with the correct grammar and vocabulary. This is a different skill altogether and will therefore require preparation beyond the Scribble Technique.

## How to Revise on your Own

Preparation for these exams can best be described using the 'meal analogy'. To produce a meal, you need to gather the ingredients, cook it using the recipe and then present it nicely. Revising for 'written prose' is analogous in the following way:

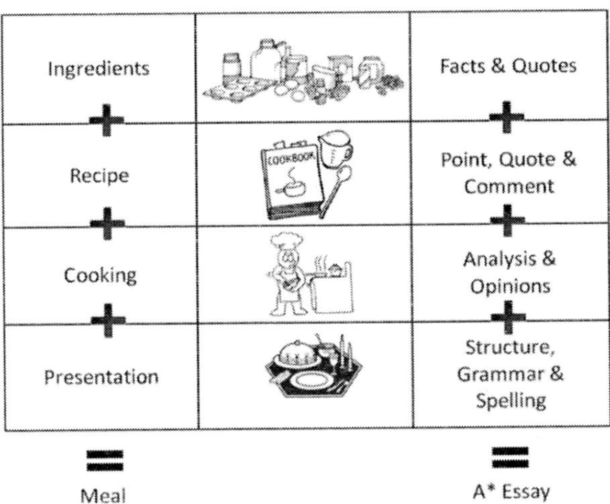


**Ingredients**: Learning the Facts

For degrees like History and Politics, examiners often ask you to use the 'source and your **knowledge**' to answer questions. The 'knowledge' part requires learning facts prior to the exam. As you probably guessed, the Scribble Technique® can take care of this. Completing 2 or 3 layers of your learning pack should do the job.

**Recipe**: Point, Quote and Comment

You've probably heard a lot about 'Point, Quote and Comment' (PQC). However, if you haven't, PQC is the best method or recipe to use when answering exam questions for these subjects. The table below summarises what PQC is:

| Key Area | What is it? | Example |
|---|---|---|
| Point | State a relevant point which helps directly answer the question. | Lenny was too innocent to comprehend loneliness. |
| Quote | Provide a quote or some evidence to back up your statement. | *"Tha's good,"* he said. *"You drink some, George. You take a good big drink."* He smiled happily. |
| Comment | Explain what the quote or evidence shows. | George has just reamed Lennie out for drinking too fast, but Lennie is so innocent that he doesn't even get mad. He just smiles 'happily' when George takes a drink. From this perspective, innocence doesn't look too bad. |

It's important to practice using PQC. When interviewing students who've achieved top marks in written prose subjects, like English Literature, many recommended using PQC and checking with tutors. This is a very useful iterative process because tutors can show how you can tweak answers to increase exam marks.

**Cooking**: Analysing and Generating Opinions

Before using PQC to answer exam questions, you'll need to analyse texts and generate opinions. This can be tricky and some people are naturally more opinionated than others. I still remember my GCSE English Literature class at high school when I sat next to my friend Iona. The teacher would get us to read an extract from the book, 'Of Mice and Men', ask us a question and give us five minutes to write down an answer. On one occasion, our teacher asked us a very basic question:

"Why are George and Lenny friends?"

In five minutes, I wrote about seven lines containing one or two PQCs. In that same period, Iona wrote over thirty lines with six PQCs! How did she generate so many opinions on a relationship between two fictional characters!? Out of frustration, I approached the teacher at the end of the class and asked:

*"Do you ever find that you just don't have an opinion? When you asked that question, all I could really think of was that George and Lenny were friends because they liked each other and got on. My mind went blank after that!"*

She said that by reading the book a few times and participating in class, I'll naturally start forming good opinions. This never happened! Only after college and first year university did I find a way to enhance the opinion generating part of my brain.

To prepare for my 'Written prose' subjects at university, I immersed myself in the subject material and case studies. I used the Scribble Technique® to learn the material on each page and then immediately forced myself to analyse and generate opinions on the subject. It didn't matter how daft my opinion was, I wrote it down. Often exploring one avenue of thought can lead to better roads, if you simply ask 'why?'. For example, Lenny and George were friends because they liked each other and got on – why?

Lenny likes how George looks out for him and George finds his innocence endearing – why?

George knows that Lenny is a good person at heart but isn't intelligent. People try to take advantage of this; George takes pride in defending Lenny from bullies. He's a big brother to him. Lenny also knows that he needs George to protect him and get him out of trouble. – why?

I called this procedure '5 whys', inspired by the method used by Toyota factories in Japan to identify core problems in their manufacturing process. With written prose subjects, '5 whys' can help you home in on your core opinions.

After two layers using the Scribble Technique® along with '5 whys', I had a strong memory bank filled with both facts and opinions. This meant that in the exam, all I had to do was merge those opinions together and present them coherently.

**Presentation**: Essay Structure, Spelling and Grammar

Answers in your exams need a to have structure. Be sure to spend 5 minutes jotting down an essay plan before answering each exam question.

**Written Prose: What to do in Lectures?**

If you can't generate opinions easily or 'blag', go to lectures and participate. During my Management classes at university, I took my written opinions in with me and voiced them out loud. Immediately, I could tell if it was a good opinion or not by the reaction of those around me and the lecturer. Very often, other people would either build on my opinion or counter it. I'd add all this to my opinion bank!

Written prose subjects are unique in that the exam marks are subjective to the marker. Your lecturers will probably be the ones marking your exam, so capturing their opinions and analysis about commonly assessed case studies or topics would be a good idea.

**In Summary:**

| **Subject Type** | **Exam Preparation** |
|---|---|
| Fact Recall | 2-3 layers using the Scribble Technique<br>+ Past Papers |
| Method & Understanding | Total number of practice questions completed $\propto$ Exam mark<br>+ Past Papers |
| Written Prose | 2-3 layers using the Scribble Technique to learn facts<br>Use '5 Whys' to generate opinions<br>+ Past Papers |

# Chapter 18

# The Ultimate University Game Plan in Steps

**Step 1:** Build your network of specialists – lecturers, older students and peers.

**Step 2:** What to study? Assemble your learning packs ASAP.

**Step 3:** Use your learning packs to calculate when you should start preparing for exams and set your timetable.

**Step 4:** Identify your subject types – fact recall, method and understanding or written prose?

**Step 5:** Begin your layered learning using the correct study techniques.

| | **Exam preparation** | |
|---|---|---|
| **Subject type** | **Primary revision techniques** | **Secondary revision techniques** |
| Fact recall | Scribble Technique + past papers | Mind mapping, picture association and mnemonics |
| Method & understanding | Practice questions + past papers | |
| Written prose | Scribble Technique + essay practice using '5 whys' + past papers | |

From layered learning, to picking your learning resources, to the Scribble Technique® and everything in between, blending these together is crucial to achieving top grades. The details are important, but it's equally important to understand the bigger picture:

**Revision isn't some casual learning process. It should be more industrial. Your study room at university or at home should feel like a factory where every time you sit down to work, the factory turns on and information starts being processed and stored in your brain. It's your job to design the factory in an efficient way and equip it with the right tools so that the process of learning is done quickly and effectively.**

By reading through this chapter, you have equipped your factory with the best tools in the business – so use them!

# Motivation – Getting to the Table and Staying There

In theory, achieving top grades is simple. You make a reasonable plan and you work on it until you realise your ambitions. We both know that but actually turning our thoughts into actions can be very difficult. Procrastinating is easy and focusing for extended periods of time is hard. What can we do to improve?

We've already touched on using a gamified learning process to stay focused and keep work interesting. Are there other ways we can keep ourselves motivated? Can we change our mind-set so that we don't need to motivate ourselves? How do ultra-productive people think and behave? What techniques can we use to increase our stamina and attention span? I'll answer these questions and more over the next few chapters.

# Chapter 19
# **Your Hologram**

You are standing at the bottom of a staircase that represents your future. The staircase is long, filled with various obstacles and has a hologram of your future self ahead of you. This hologram represents your fantasies and dreams; it is a depiction of where you see yourself in the near future.

**The brighter, exciting and more vivid your hologram is, the easier it will be to move up the staircase.**

Throughout my life so far, there have been periods of time where this hologram was uninspiring and boring. There were also times when it was exciting and vivid, such as during second year college and the last 2 years of university. The latter periods were those where I didn't have to motivate myself and worked consistently without having to push myself too hard. Working hard felt normal and I was on autopilot. What was the difference between these periods of time? Where did my desires come from? What changed my hologram? It's difficult to answer these questions as there were many factors at play but both of my most productive and successful periods during education came as a result of influence from older mentors.

## Enhancing your Hologram

My second year at college was one of my most successful years, partly because the sting of my bad grades left me with a real chip on my shoulder to prove everyone wrong, but mainly because of a mentor I met after results day. There was one conversation in particular which triggered a massive change in my attitude.

Over a short chat, he described how he improved his grades over one year and secured a place at his first-choice university. He then painted this incredible picture of university life which in hindsight was probably a little exaggerated, but at the time I believed every word. He spoke about his job in investment banking, his salary and overall life after university. I left the conversation thinking, 'I want all of that!'. Ever since that day, I couldn't stop fantasising about university life and had this reccurring vision of being just like him. My hologram turned from a dull projection into a bright and exciting auricle! This triggered a series of positive changes. My motivation went through the roof, bad habits went out of the window and grades started improving.

My hologram didn't change as a result of an inspirational YouTube video, self-help book or seminar. It came from speaking with individuals who I admired and related to.

**If you have a clear vision of your future self and can understand the connection from that all the way down to the specific work you're doing at any given moment, you never have to worry about motivating yourself.**

**What if you don't have a mentor?**

**Melissa:** *"I know that I want to do a postgraduate course, but it doesn't excite me in the way your vision excites you."*

**Me:** *"What about going to an American university? Surely that excites you – have you been to visit the universities?"*

**Melissa:** *"Yes – that's just an idea at the moment but it does excite me. I haven't visited them."*

**Me:** *"You don't sound very excited about it – you should save up and book a flight to America! Go alone, visit the campuses and speak to as many people as you can. You will come back with a clear vision and a fire up your a**! It will be the best money you've ever spent."*

Melissa followed my advice and travelled to the States. She contacted undergrads at various universities and one girl generously let her stay in her dorm room – gotta love Americans! She made new friends and experienced what life was like there. Unsurprisingly, she came back with a raging fire in her belly. I could see it in her eyes and the way she spoke about the trip. Her hologram had changed.

**Your Friends**

Your friends can influence your work ethic and motivation in a different way to an older mentor. As I mentioned before, I was one of four people who were awarded with a Dean's list certificate and the other three were my closest friends. This was no coincidence. We continuously influenced each other's habits in a very subtle way without even realising it at the time. You may feel like you are an independent thinker, however, your choices are being nudged and prodded by those around you.

These choices include, 'Should I work or play?' You are going to ask yourself this question thousands of times while at university. For arguments sake, let's say this question will pop into your head exactly 1000 times between now and your final year exams. If your closest friends are quite laid back and reactive then you'll probably end up choosing 'play' 600 to 700 times. However, if your friends are inherently ambitious and have a hunger to succeed, this will rub off on you whether you want it to or not. As a result, you'll probably end up choosing 'work' 600 to 700 times. This is a big edge!

Your friends can also be your mentors. Even though Danny was my peer, I looked up to him because he had many of the characteristics that I wanted, and I was open about that to him. He and other close friends shaped my hologram just as much as my older mentors did.

**Your Hologram**

When you close your eyes and think about your future self, do you see anything? Or are you striking a blank? Do you struggle to get out of bed and motivate yourself to complete work? If so, find yourself an older mentor.

Keep your eyes peeled, get out there and speak to people. This means saying 'yes' when your parents tell you to call someone because they 'can help you'. It means, mingling with people from the year above or going to careers events and asking questions like:

*"What advice would you give someone in my position?"*

*"What do you do on a day-to-day basis at work?"*

*"Do you enjoy what you do?"*

*"How did you get on at university and did your marks help you get a job?"*

If everyone understood the power a single experience or conversation could have on their life, you would never see anyone hiding in the corner on their phone.

# Chapter 20
# Obstacles

Still using the staircase analogy, as you make your way towards your goal, there will be some obstacles in your way. Most of these will be illusions that you've conjured up in your own mind. These represent your insecurities and personal beliefs about your own ability. We all have them! Some obstacles will be real; these represent external factors that you have limited control over, such as your course structure or choice of subjects. Knowing and accepting what you can and can't control is crucial to achieving your final goal.

**I'm Not Smart Enough**

Intelligence is a word that's thrown around a lot. Here is the official definition of it and the one I am referring to from this point onwards:

*The ability to acquire and apply knowledge and skills*
- *Oxford Dictionary*

Yes, there are different types of intelligence, such as social intelligence which is the ability to read peoples' behaviour. However, the intelligence I'm referring to is the one that helps you learn and understand new information – the one that helps you achieve good grades.

## Intelligence vs. Hard Work

Prior to college, whenever I failed a test or exam, I entered an internal debate, one that was filled with self-doubt and punishing questions about my ability. Was it my intelligence, was it because I was lazy? My thought process went something like this:

*"Syed did well without putting much effort in – so maybe I'm just a bit thick?"*

*"Then again, I spent 2 days playing video games. If I worked instead, I would have probably earned an A."*

*"On the last mock exam, I didn't play video games and worked hard but still ended up with a D – it's definitely my intelligence. It's mum and dad's fault for my crappy genes!"*

This internal debate went on and on right up until my first-year results at college. That's when I decided that I'd had enough! Part of the reason I started working like crazy after this was to put this intelligence vs. hard work debate to bed. That's when I told myself:

"*Right - if I do every single question in this Mechanics 1 textbook and still don't get an A then it will prove that I'm not intelligent.*"

Over the remainder of the summer holidays I kept my word and completed every single question in that textbook. During class, I noticed an improvement in my ability to answer questions and was doing well in my homework. However, failing so much in the past had made me sceptical and I still didn't believe I was intelligent enough to match my high performing peers.

As the exam period approached, and with multiple retakes, I had only one day to recap my maths mechanics module. I was worried that I would forget all the content I'd spent the last few weeks memorising, after all, it was several months ago! The exam went well but in the days running up to results day I was sceptical. In the queue to pick up the results I was even more sceptical. As the teacher licked her finger and flicked through to find my results I was still sceptical, but:

A big "A" stared back at me and ended that scepticism in an instant.

I was shocked! Many of my subject marks were above 90%, including the maths mechanics module. To those who are naturally intelligent and believe in themselves, these grades won't be a big deal. However, as someone who was unsure of himself for so many years, these grades eradicated years of insecurity.

The moment I saw that results sheet, I stopped using intelligence as an excuse and realised that I was in control of my future. I left college that day knowing what it felt like to believe in yourself. This triumph is etched in my memory, and whenever I'm feeling unsure about myself, I think of those few months in college where I backed myself and won.

Fast forward a few years, I am now the founder of Academic Underdogs and an academic coach. I speak to people as old as 30 who still don't know what it's like to 'believe in yourself'. Many still blame their intelligence; some openly acknowledge that they are inherently flawed in some way and have given up on achieving their goals altogether. Some show confidence in public but privately feel that successful people have some kind of X-factor that they will never obtain. If you also doubt yourself in this way, I hope my story helps you re-think your assumptions.

**Do we Need Intelligence to Achieve Top Grades?**

For many pursuits/careers, above average intelligence will give you a big edge. It'll have an immediate and obvious impact on your success and your salary if you work in the financial, healthcare or educational sector, but it will also give you an edge in many other careers. The more intelligent you are, the more likely you are to get a promotion and to get a read on your employers/colleagues.

However, when it comes to academic success, hard-work and study technique trump intelligence every day of the week. Having beaten many people more intelligent than me in both college and university, I'm living proof that you don't need intelligence to achieve good grades!

Despite my efforts to convince people, many of my mentees still find themselves cursing their intelligence. This is like complaining about the sky being blue! Yes, your intelligence can improve, but it happens very slowly and there is no pill you can swallow to double your IQ. If you can accept that your intelligence is a constant (in the short-term), you can then focus on improving your variables like your ability to concentrate.

*"The measure of our future success and happiness will not be the quality of the cards we are dealt by unseen hands, but the poise and wisdom with which we play them. Choose to play each hand to the best of your ability without wasting the time or energy it takes to complain about either the cards or the dealer or the often unfair rules of the game. Play both the winning and the losing hands as best you can, then fold the cards and ante up for the next deal!"*
*- Joe Klock*

**I Can't Concentrate**

Being able to sit down at your desk each day and get some work done for a few hours doesn't sound very difficult. However, for some reason, most of us find it difficult to get going and often drift into LaLa Land after just a few lines.

At one point, I was convinced that I had ADD (Attention Deficit Disorder) a psychological condition that prevents you from concentrating. In fact, I went to the doctor to check, but my suspicions were wrong. Even after this check-up, I still felt my poor attention span was completely out of my control and that I'd need a miracle to ever get anything done. This was far from true! I see the same complaints every year on Twitter – does this look familiar?…

**Demise Swift** @demislouises
I'm too tired to do coursework or revise. #Sleepy #Tired #ThinkImAnaemic #NeedMoreIron

**Elijah Ofon** @elixofon
How am I supposed to concentrate after such a long day? Don't they understand!!?" #Bed #NeedForSleep #NeedForSleep2

We're all familiar with that tired and 'groggy' feeling where an attempt to read a few lines of your textbook turns into a daydream. It's almost as if our minds run on batteries. Every morning we wake up with a finite amount of energy for the day. When it runs out, intense thinking is no longer possible and only sleep can recharge the battery.

Let's do this!

R.I.P

## Can we Change our Attention Span and Battery Life?

Attention spans and energy levels can be improved gradually by pushing yourself to do a little more than you did the previous day. This will enhance your study stamina. To make this a little clearer, let's use the analogy of Stacey the marathon runner:

Stacey decided to run a 10km marathon in 9 months' time. Having never completed this distance before, she began training hard and on her first day recorded a distance of 2km in 50 mins before running out of energy. She felt disappointed and began thinking she wasn't cut out for running. However, she decided to keep trying. For days, she struggled – 1.9km:51 mins; 2km:54 mins; 1.8km: 52 mins. On the fourth day, she got herself to 1.8km in 49 minutes. She felt like her energy was running out again but somehow found a way to push on to finish at 2.1km in 51 mins. By constantly pushing herself to run a little further and faster each time, she built up her stamina to a point where she could complete the 10km marathon in good time.

## Is Training for Athletics Different from Revising for an Exam?

It took me years to realise this, but our minds are just like muscles that can be conditioned to last longer and work more effectively. Just how Stacey pushed to do an extra 100m, you can push to do one more page or one more question. Over time you'll be able to work for longer periods of time without feeling 'groggy' all the time. In the next chapter, I'll show you how to improve your attention span and stamina by creating your own performance metrics.

## My Lecturers are Rubbish

Many professors are excellent thinkers and pioneers in their field of study but can fall short as teachers. This is unfortunate, because they are more important and relevant than your teachers at high school and college. However, they are still only one tool in the toolbox. Just because you have a bad lecturer doesn't mean you're doomed!

One of my lecturers was Hungarian and had a very strong accent that everyone found difficult to understand. As a result, most people didn't see the point of going to his lectures and he'd be lucky if half the year group turned up. Instead of writing him off like everyone else, I learnt a few simple Hungarian words and used them in a conversation with him. He loved it! From that point onwards, all my e-mails were answered within a day or two and he noticeably had more time to help me with coursework. You cannot control which professors you get but you can somewhat control what you get out of them.

## Thought Tracking

"I'm not smart enough."

"My professor can't teach this course to save his life."

"I am incapable of concentrating for longer than 3 minutes."

"I can't motivate myself."

As you start studying after a long day, these are some of the many insecurities and thoughts that will enter your head without invitation. When you're standing at the edge of your attention span and the WhatsApp icon on your phone is pulsating, one of these thoughts will turn up and push you over the edge. Next thing you know, you waste the next half-hour in a group chat about Love Island and enter a downward spiral of procrastination! This is why you need to manage your thoughts and continuously disprove your insecurities over and over again. I've found that tracking these thoughts and writing them down keeps them at bay. Below there is an example of how I do this.

Exams were a few months away and I was working on my first layer for an Organic Chemistry module in my room. This part of the course was 'fact heavy', so I was working through the course handouts using the Scribble Technique®. My goal was to complete pages 23 to 26 in half an hour. My desk had the Organic Chemistry handouts, a paper pad, pen and a piece of paper to track my progress over the half-hour. When the clock hit 12:30 PM, I had finished all 5 pages and my progress tracking sheet looked like this:

Target: Pages 23 – 31 by 12:30 PM

~~People - Rosh~~
~~People - Mum~~
**Pg 23 √**

~~People - Rosh~~
~~Lect - tool box~~
~~Intel - AS~~
~~Idea~~
**Pg 24 √**
~~People - Mum~~
~~Conc - Athlete~~
**Pg 25 √**

~~Idea~~
~~People - Rosh~~
~~Fail - A-level~~
**Pg 26 √**

These were all the obstacles that popped into my head without invitation while trying to complete 4 pages. As I was working through page 23, I started thinking about an argument I had with my flatmate. As soon as I caught myself thinking about this, I wrote it down and got back into the content. After doing 2 rounds of the Scribble Technique, my mum popped into my head because she recently had a worrying biopsy test. Again, I wrote it down and jumped back in. As you can see, many of my obstacles revolve around people and yours probably will as well.

There were also other familiar appearances! During page 24, I had trouble understanding a concept and remembered that my friend had gotten it straightaway. This made me feel insecure about my intelligence. However, as soon as I caught myself going down this road, I reminded myself of my A-Level grades and how intelligence doesn't matter. This shut down the insecurity and I got back to work.

Always use past triumphs and memories to help you squash your insecurities.

Some thoughts are harmless distractions, but these should also be tracked. For example, during page 26 I thought of a business idea to help university students find work experience. Instead of daydreaming about how much I was going to charge everyone and what my logo should look like, I wrote the business idea down in a special folder on my phone and then got back to work.

All this might sound a bit daft, however, both myself and many of my mentors have had great results using this 'thought tracking' method. I still practice it to this day. In fact, as I'm writing this, there is a note window open with 4 distractions logged!

# Chapter 21
# **Moving Forward**

Your bright and exciting hologram is showing you the way and pulling you towards your ambitions like the ring did to Frodo. You are fully aware of the obstacles in front of you; you understand what you can and cannot change and are able to manage internal distractions. Now all you need to do is move forward. Take it one step, one hour, one day and one week at a time until you get the results that you seek.

Achieving top grades is a lot like winning the Premier League, in that teams can either win, lose or draw and the team that consistently performs the best ultimately wins the league. Every day, week and month from now until your exams is an important match that you have to prepare for, because every time you underprepare you underperform, and when you underperform your chances of achieving your goals diminish.

The more good days you have and the fewer bad days you have, the better your grades will be. Simple! That begs one question: How do you have more good days?

By understanding every element of your study cycle and then improving it.

**What is the Study Cycle?**

Eat, sleep, study, repeat – the study cycle is a routine you participate in every day. It has 3 parts: intent, action and maintenance:

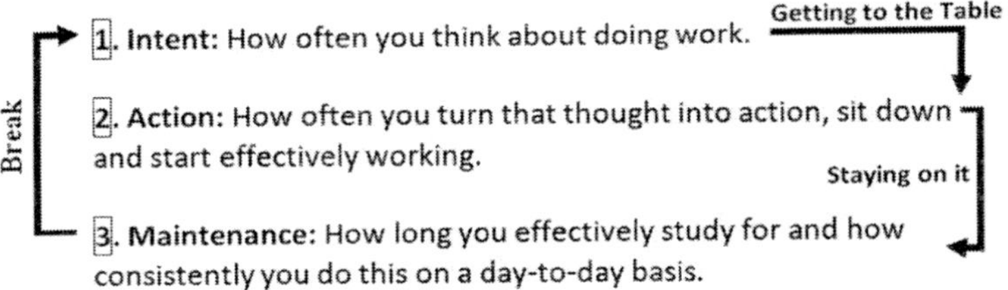


If you're reading this book, you undoubtedly have plenty of intent and probably think about studying a great deal. After all, it's easy to think about what you should be doing. However, acting on your intentions is harder and requires a greater amount of willpower and energy. After you've sat down at your desk and pushed through the first 5-10 minutes, doesn't it feel a lot easier to keep going? The graph below shows how each element of the study cycle requires different levels of willpower and mental energy.

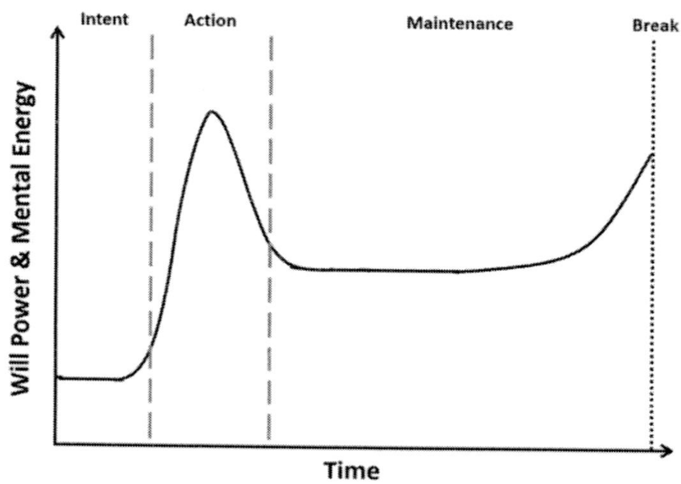


After getting over the first hump, it becomes much easier to concentrate for 15-20 minutes. As you near the end of your attention span, it becomes harder to concentrate and you will need a break. This is how your mind operates during the study cycle and understanding this will help you improve. Remind yourself of this graph every time you feel like procrastinating. It's only the first 5-10 minutes which are difficult!

Now that you fully understand what the study cycle is, we are ready to learn how we can be effective in executing each of the three elements. I've experimented with ***hundreds*** of tricks, hacks and techniques to ensure my study cycle runs like a brand-new Ferrari and not a banged-up Skoda. Let's begin by discussing the most important technique – goal setting.

## Goal Setting (the proper way)

[Target study cycle elements: **1**, **2** and **3**]

Goal setting is a powerful process for identifying your ideal future and motivating yourself to turn this into reality. I'm going to provide a new perspective on effective goal setting. Let's first get the 4 main rules out of the way:

### 4 Golden Rules

Each goal should be:

1. **Written Down**

Your mind can easily twist, bend and extend goals as time goes by. Writing something down affirms it and makes it tangible. To change that goal would mean physically crossing it out or throwing it in the bin. Not the most comfortable thing to do!

2. **Clear**

The goal should be so clear that you know immediately whether you have successfully accomplished it. A pass or fail statement such as 'complete 25 practice questions in my maths textbook by 15:00' is much more defined than 'work on maths for rest of the day'. Keep them black and white.

### 3. Made with a Plan and Deadline

*"A dream is just a dream. A goal is a dream with a plan and a deadline."*

- *Anonymous*

Having a plan and deadline will provide structure to the goal. Furthermore, a good game plan will reduce self-doubt and prevent feeling insecure about being able to complete what you need on time.

### 4. Realistic

There is no point setting yourself unrealistic goals because you will constantly underachieve and lack confidence in your ability. The goal should be ambitious but within reach so that you are able to follow it through and gain confidence from completing it.

Try and stick to these rules so you can get the most out of your goals. Now, let's talk about setting goals across time frames.

## Goal Time Frames

Goal setting across multiple time frames will help improve all three elements of your study cycle.

| Goal | Time span | Example |
|---|---|---|
| Long term | Years | I will achieve a First in my degree by this time next year |
| Medium term | Weeks/Days | Complete first layer of module 1 in two weeks |
| Short term | Hours | Practice questions 1 to 5 – by 14:00 |

**Long-term Goals**

These should be set before the start of each academic year and never change. Even now, after university and starting my business, all the long-term goals I've ever made are printed out and stuck on my wall:

- I will achieve at least 3A's in my A-Levels by June 2006 √

- I will achieve a First-Class Honours in my Degree by June 2009 √

- I will be accepted on to an Internship Program at an Investment Bank by June 2009 √

- I will write a book to show A-level students how to improve their grades by December 2013 √

- I will write a book to show GCSE students how to improve their grades by March 2015 √

- I will establish a profitable e-commerce business generating £x per year in revenue by April 2017 √

- I will write a book to show university students how to improve their grades and become more charismatic by August 2019 √

Every time a goal was achieved, I would draw a large tick on the page and every time a goal expired without me achieving it, I either extended it or wrote a new one. I recommend doing the same: write or print your long-term goals out in large, bold font on A4 paper. Then, stick them up right in front of your desk.

Finally, give yourself a small print or a disclaimer on those goals to help keep the goal fresh, something like:

**I know this goal will try and fade away over time, but I must try and fight to keep it close**

It's all well and good writing what you want on a piece of paper. However, you need to genuinely want to achieve the goals you set for yourself. One university student I mentored told me he wanted to achieve a First (70%+) in his degree. He took my advice, wrote this goal down and pinned it up in his work area. At the end of his academic year and after his last exam, I asked him how he got on and he replied "Yes, OK, I suppose. I should have passed." This clearly showed that, at some point during the year, his goal changed from 70% (First) to 40% (A pass). If he genuinely wanted those grades, he would have been kicking and screaming over not achieving what he set out to do.

**Medium-term Goals**

Goals across weeks and days will help you piece together the long-term plan. Set the goals to give you some room to manoeuvre in case it takes longer than expected. Once these goals are set, you can gauge whether you're working hard enough to complete layers in time for the exam and adjust your time accordingly.

As a final note, when setting goals for the day it's best to get your least favourite pieces of work out of the way first when you're fresh and motivation is high. It will help you build momentum and continue with the rest of the day.

**Accountability**

For goals in any time frame, sharing them with your parents or friends makes you accountable for getting them done. This is an effective way of motivating yourself to achieve what you set out to do and it can create a little competition between you and your friends!

History has shown how intense rivalry between people can exponentially improve the skillset of those involved. This is true in academia, politics and sports. Federer, Nadal, Djokovic and Murray have improved their tennis as a result of intense competition between each other. Cristiano Ronaldo openly admitted that his rivalry with Lionel Messi greatly improved his game.

We are all inherently competitive and want to win. When you go to the gym and jump on a treadmill, don't you immediately feel the need to run faster and longer than the person next to you? The feeling is magnified when you go for a run with a friend. The same applies to academic study. However, as studying is an individual task, you have to create the competition yourself!

This can be done using a weekly e-mail. For example, every Monday you and a friend can send each other's performance for the week ahead and evaluate the week at the end. Even though you know your friends won't say anything or judge you if you're slacking, a natural competitive tendency will push you to be better than them. The mere thought of someone else knowing you have underachieved will get you over the line every week.

### Short-term Goals Using Performance Tracking

[Target study cycle elements: **1**, **2** & **3**]

At this moment in time academia is your sport. It is by no means a sexy sport. No one in Hollywood is making inspiring movies about it and Ryan Gosling/Emma Stone are not waiting in the wings to play you. There is no show on Netflix about the trials and tribulations of Jimmy, a student trying to pass his exams, with epic montages of endless study sessions filled with Wotsit and Monster Energy binges. Nevertheless, our exam is our tournament and study cycle is our training. We should train like a top athlete would and look to them for inspiration whenever we're feeling down.

One of the aspects we can borrow from top athletes is performance tracking. Let's take Olympic gold medallist Mo Farah as an example. He and his team track everything from body-fat percentage to lap times. They can tell you how he is performing on the track, what food he is consuming and what his mental state is on any given day. As academic athletes, what metrics should we use to track our day-to-day progress? These are what I used:

1. Number of A4 pages learned using the Scribble Technique® per hour/day/week.
2. Total time spent working per day/week.
3. Average attention span (I use a stop clock).
4. Total number of distracting thoughts during self-study periods.
5. Past papers percentage marks.

Even as I'm writing this, I have a notes tab open showing how many words I've written today and every day for the past 6 weeks. I've noted down when I started writing and when I stopped, then calculated how many words I'd done per hour on average. When I wake up the next morning, my goal is very simple: **To beat my previous days' score.**

Approaching your study cycle in this way will help you focus on your short-term results and reduce anxiety caused by longer term fears like, 'What if I fail?' You will become a results oriented person who not only makes goals and pushes to achieve them, but also craves the feeling of achieving them again and again.



## Self-bribery

[Target study cycle elements: **2** and **3**]

Sounds a bit childish, right? But bribing yourself is a useful way of providing an extra push to hit your short time-frame targets. It will also help to condition yourself into being a results driven person who looks forward to finishing tasks thoroughly and detests leaving things half done. Additionally, bribes and treats can be incorporated into the goals you set at the start of the day.

For example:

Last 10 pages of this textbook = 15 min break and sandwich snack.

First 20 questions of maths = 30 min Game of Thrones.

It is important to ensure that the treats you choose don't let you get carried away and cause you to waste more time than you accounted for. It goes without saying that you should avoid anything that can make your task more difficult, such as alcohol. When you're taking a break, it is much easier to say 10 more minutes of TV then it is to say 10 more minutes of essay writing.

Below are 5 of the best and worst things that you can do during your break. You'll see that even though the 'worst' may seem more fun, they will deter you from getting back to revision. You need to give yourself treats according to the time of day and how much work you've done

<u>5 Best:</u>

1) Short burst of intensive exercise - 10 min sit ups
2) Short walk or fresh air
3) Small snack
4) Shower
5) Short TV programme

<u>5 worst:</u>

1) Heavy meal
2) Starting a movie
3) Shopping
4) YouTube
5) PS4, Xbox or other games console

## High Impact – High Reward

[Target study cycle elements: **1** and **2**]

Have you ever experienced a time when you just couldn't build any momentum? Every time you attempted to work, it all goes square and nothing gets done? Me too.

The damage comes when the 'slow patch' continues and then becomes the norm or a habit. Therefore, it's important to be aware when it happens and to take action. Taking action can sometimes be hard but with three simple steps, you should be able to get over the hill.

> **Step One:** Recognise whether something is a one-off or if it is turning into a spiralling habit.
>
> **Step Two:** Have the discipline to make a personal change to break that habit. The longer you leave it running the harder it will be to break.

**Step Three:** Take action by doing something out of your comfort zone, such as something you would not normally do.

After successfully completing my mid-year exams I decided to take a break for 2 weeks. Following a few nights out, I attempted to build momentum and get back into a routine. I was too complacent, though, and it just wasn't happening. This continued for another 2 weeks until a friend helped me realise that continuing in this way would undo all my hard work in the first term. I'm glad I took the break and I really needed it, but I had to find a way to get back into a routine.

As a 'punishment' for myself I took my books, told my girlfriend to leave me alone for a couple of days, got my mum to take my phone, drop me to my grandma's house and just leave me there for a few days. Looking back makes me both cringe and chuckle. My grandma was a very spiritual lady who meditated for hours on end. I hoped that by staying there, I could soak-up some of that spirituality and it would somehow help me break out of my cycle. It felt like I was going on my very own revision spiritual retreat and guess what? It worked! While I didn't turn into a meditating teenager, over those few days I worked efficiently, hit all my goals and got right back on track.

Back then I was kind of spooked and thought that the spirituality helped me change course. In hindsight, it was the random shift in environment, boredom (no TV) and early starts because my grandma kept waking me up with all her bell ringing and chanting. Regardless, these factors caused enough of a high impact to change my destructive habit and get right back on course.

You should never underestimate the power of a change of scenery, especially if it comes with a change in your daily rhythms.

## David Attenborough is in my Head

[Target study cycle elements: **3**]

This is a weird but effective technique for when you are close to hitting your target but running low on concentration. To grab those last few minutes of your attention span, use your mind to narrate the information in your textbook or learning pack using someone else's voice. This could be anyone's voice but personally I like using David Attenborough's! I find his voice quite distinctive and it makes me want to listen to what he's saying. Have a go – no harm in trying!

## Ejection Seat (coming close to something then bailing at the last moment)

[Target study cycle elements: **2**]

This little trick can help you avoid procrastination. It should be used when you need to start working and there is something you are really tempted to do, such as watching a YouTube video, reading a magazine, or playing a video game. Bring yourself close to doing it and then bail at the last minute – like how a fighter pilot ejects before crashing. The more emphatically you do this, the better! For example, if you want to watch Netflix, pick up your phone, open Netflix but then emphatically chuck it on your bed and immediately go to your desk! I know this sounds ridiculous and weird but you would be surprised at how often it works.

### Start-Ask-Do

[Target study cycle elements: **1**]

"How do you get so much done so quickly?"

I was handing in my final year design project when my friend asked me this question. I had just received an internship offer from one of the top investment banks in the city and had come a long way from my feeble first year.

I answered, "With every piece of work, I start almost immediately – even if it's to an attempt a question or word vomit a few paragraphs of an essay. This gives me a feeling for what is required."

"Then I ask myself: what is the easiest way I can get this done? And I find an answer."

"When I have a plan, I use every hack and technique I know to make the task interesting and to ensure I focus 100% until it is done."

It seems a little counterintuitive to start without planning, but you'll be surprised how many people deliberate over when to start; how to start; and why to start, only to lose interest in the task altogether. Start without thinking like it's a knee-jerk reaction. Your writing doesn't have to be pretty, coherent or grammatically correct. Just get it out. As the ideas start flowing, you will seamlessly move into the 'maintenance' phase of the study cycle.

It's easy to underestimate your own ability. When I was set a piece of coursework that had a massive equation on it or complex question, I assumed that it would take some hefty reading before I could even attempt it. Quite often, I was able to answer some of the questions and sometimes complete the whole assignment just from the information I remembered from a lecture.

Ever since university, 'start-ask-do' has been my motto and I use it with every task I set, including this book! When I first decided to write this series, I opened a word document, titled it, *How to ACE University* and word vomited 2000 words in fifteen minutes. Had I tried to google similar books, ask friends about my idea or try to create a chapter structure, it would have wasted time and sent the project to the death spiral of my 'do it later' list.

Whether it's a job application, a piece of graded coursework, an exam revision or a weight loss goal – start first and think later!

## Other Tips

Here are some hints on what you can do to maximise your work rate:

1. **Regularly Change Environment**: After a few hours of working in the same spot it's helpful to move somewhere else. Psychologically you will be 'starting afresh'. I personally like spending one half of the day at home and then walking to the library to finish the rest.

2. **Avoid Heavy Meals**: You will feel tired and be less productive after a large meal because all the blood rushes from your head to your stomach.

3. **Downtime**: Our minds don't work too well when there's a load of emotional churning going on. When you're exhausted at the end of each day do something that lowers your stress such as exercise, TV, video games or talking with friends.

4. **Work Under Bright White or Blue Light**: There are two main types of indoor lighting: bright white and warm white. Warm white is generally used for living conditions to create comfortable 'easy on the eyes' lighting, while bright light is used in offices to imitate daylight conditions and increase productivity. Try and work during daylight hours or in places where there are bright white lights.

5. **Listen to Gaming Music While Working**: These are designed to keep people focused.

## Hide your phone

[Target study cycle elements: **3**]

Question: What contains a bunch of distractions and follows you around everywhere? You guessed it – your smartphone. With all the games, instant messaging and social media apps, becoming addicted to your phone is not difficult. Above all, the instant messaging apps like WhatsApp prove to be the top distractions.

This is because app designers have made us feel uncomfortable when there is information on our phones that we have not seen yet. Do you get uncomfortable about having the little star or the 'unread' symbol on the top right of your Instagram, Twitter or WhatsApp icons?

If you find it hard not to click on unread posts/messages/ tweets, then you're addicted to social information. As your concentration fades during study time, you become more susceptible to procrastination and seeing the blinking light or push notification on your phone is all it takes to break your concentration. Do yourself a favour and switch your phone off before you start working. Hand it to a friend – out of sight, out of mind. Doing this alone could improve your exam marks by 10% minimum!

**Moving Forward**

All the methods above are those I've used personally. I understand that some of them sound strange. In fact, when I started mentally narrating my chemistry textbook in David Attenborough's voice, I thought I was going a bit loony. However, sometimes it helps to make the arduous task of studying more interesting. Try them out yourself and don't be afraid to experiment with your own ideas.

# Chapter 22
# Motivation Summary

| | |
|---|---|
| Enhance your hologram | - Network with older students<br>- Build close relationships with peers you admire |
| Manage internal and external obstacles | - Establish what you can/can't control<br>- Use thought tracking |
| Keep your study cycle efficient | - Gamify your learning process<br>- Goal setting<br>- Self-bribery<br>- High impact – high reward<br>- David Attenborough is in my head<br>- Ejection seat<br>- Start-ask-do<br>- Regularly change environment<br>- Avoid heavy meals<br>- Work under bright white or blue light<br>- Listen to gaming music<br>- **Hide or switch off your phone** |

# Looking Ahead

Your time at university will be filled with lots of awesome moments, however, there will be some tough periods too. Whenever you feel like you can't hack it, remind yourself of how far you've come. You have already successfully made it through almost two decades of schooling and academia. You've met all those deadlines and navigated a number of exams to get this far. This is the final stretch of your educational journey and the first few steps into full blown adulthood. This will have its own challenges, but you don't need to worry about that. As of now, your goal is very simple –leave university with your head held high and with no regrets, knowing that you gave it your all.

Out of all the people I met at university, a minority of them truly ACE'd it in the way I described in this book and series. It's certainly not easy. Achieving an average degree score above 70%, landing a great graduate job all while having a social life is an extraordinary feat. However, you don't need to be an extraordinary person to accomplish this. People might directly and indirectly tell you that, 'You can't have it all', but you really can. You just need a plan that you agree with and some self-belief. I truly hope this book has provided you with both these things.

# FAQ

### Where did Melissa end up?

Melissa achieved a first-class honours degree and secured a Masters at her first-choice university in America. When I last spoke to her, she was considering either working for SpaceX or going to Australia. She still hasn't decided yet!

### I need more help. How do I contact you?

Whether you need help verifying your learning material, creating a schedule, career advice or anything else; contact us on www.AcademicUnderdogs.com.

We also offer mentorship programmes to help you succeed at university and beyond. Previous mentees have gone onto achieve top grades and built the confidence to impress in interviews. Using our network of employers, many of them have also been placed at fast growing start-ups around the world.

We do everything in our power to ensure you leave university with your head held high and hit the ground running as a graduate.

### Do you have any other books?

Yes! *How to ACE Your Degree* is book 1 of 3 in the *Level Up* series. Book 2, *How to be Admired & Respected*, shows you how to build a charismatic personality and influence others. Book 3, *How to Land Your Dream Graduate Job,* contains a 4-step plan to help you find and secure a career that's right for you.

How to be Admired & Respected

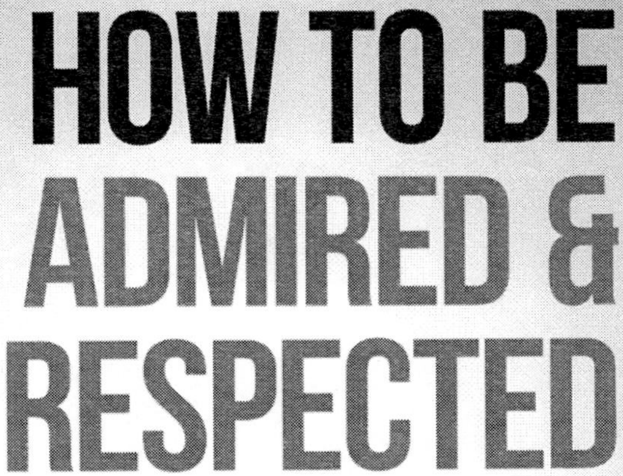


From Attracting Friends to Persuading Interviewers, We Show You How to Influence Anyone

A. RAJA

How to Land Your Dream Graduate Job